Everyday Grace

The Art of Being a Woman

Based on the Teachings of Kundalini Yoga
as taught by Yogi Bhajan®

Sat Purkh Kaur Khalsa

Kundalini F

Training 🪷 Publishing

D1410024

© 2010 Kundalini Research Institute

Published by the Kundalini Research Institute

PO Box 1819
Santa Cruz, NM 87567
www.kundaliniresearchinstitute.org
ISBN 978-1-934532-31-7

KRI Review: Siri Neel Kaur Khalsa
Consulting Editor: Nirvair Singh Khalsa
Proofreader: Sarb Jit Kaur
Index: Vanessa Khalsa
Copy Editor: Tara Joffe
Design: Prana Projects
Photography: Ravitej Singh Khalsa and Alan Miyataki
Models: Krishna Kaur, Har Rai Kaur, Guru Nam Kaur, Nirinjan Kaur Khalsa, Nicole Elliot Murray, Elan Murray, Bhajan Kaur, Suraj Kaur and Hari Darshan Kaur
Photograph of the author provided by Deborah Fryer, Lila Films, Inc.
Opening quotes from The Teachings of Yogi Bhajan: July 29, 1990 and July 13, 1979 respectively.

Everyday grace must be your reality—your norm.
—Yogi Bhajan

Nothing should shake you from the awakening art that is within you: the art of being a woman.
—*Yogi Bhajan*

To my Teacher, Yogi Bhajan, whose wisdom and compassion have opened the door for me and countless others to be graceful, beautiful, invincible women.

To my sister, Ronda, the most graceful woman I have ever known. Her kindness is her gift; her life, an inspiration; and her touch, a healing.

Contents

Grace Note

There are many different ways to think about grace—the hand of God working in your life, the gift of a teacher, or your own inner being. Throughout this book, we'll explore these notions of grace and many more. But one way to start thinking about grace is through music. A grace note is a trill or embellishment; it adds a flourish and expands on the primary tone or creates a bridge to the next primary tone. The grace note brings with it an internal rhythm, weaves itself into the melody, without taking over. In classical Indian music, there's a similar concept called *mukta,* which quite literally means "liberation." The mukta falls between two consonants and provides a little room, an internal rhythm between the words and within the words. It creates a flow. It is a grace.

Throughout the book, you'll find brief, guided meditations, *pranayams* (breathing exercises), and exercises that will serve as a kind of grace note within the flow of ideas. Take a moment to pause and reflect on these practices, or set aside time in your day to practice them in earnest. Some are simply guided visualizations and others are kriyas and meditations from the Teachings of Yogi Bhajan. Many of these grace notes are available as downloads so that you can listen to them throughout the day or practice them on the go. See the media page at www.kundaliniresearchinstitute.org.

Before you begin, bring your hands to your heart in Prayer Pose and tune in with the mantra, *Ong Namo Guru Dev Namo,* "I bow to the Infinite, I bow to the Teacher within." This will set the tone for your practice—however long or short it may be.

When grace becomes a part of you, a part of your identity, your way of being in the world, you become a part of the flow of life. You are freed—liberated—to become a part of the great mystery. Instead of wasting time and energy in trying to control everything, you can relax and enjoy life's flow. Dip your toe in the stream of life. Each moment brings a change in the river, and grace allows that change to elevate you, transform you, and "guide your way on."

Ong   Na – mo   Gu – ru   Dev   Na – mo

Chapter One

Amazing Grace

Woman is not a small thing. She is the root, she is the trunk, she is the branches, and she is the leaves of the tree of life.[1]

— *Yogi Bhajan*

I grew up singing the traditional hymn, *Amazing Grace*, most Sundays, and it remains close to my heart even today. The words, "how sweet the sound," still resound in my consciousness. Grace, as a concept, has always been appealing to me (perhaps because I needed it more than most or because I'd received more than my fair share?). That some mystery, something outside myself, might intercede on my behalf, might somehow make up for my own perceived shortcomings and make a difference in my life, especially

1 © The Teachings of Yogi Bhajan, July 7, 1978

in those times when I didn't believe I deserved it, is a beautiful idea, yes? So many paths—or dharmas—lead to grace, and I've traveled many of them, each taking me one step closer to my Self and my spirit.

One day I found myself in a Kundalini Yoga as taught by Yogi Bhajan® class, chanting "I am Grace of God." This turned everything I'd come to understand about faith and my own experience on its head. Instead of grace descending down to me from above, I was now asked to recognize that grace—that quixotic nectar, that sweetness of the sound—existed within me, as me!

Changing the definition of grace to include myself, my own nature as a woman, my being, took me a long, long way from home; yet it had also been there all along. My own mother's tremendous strength, courage, passion, and commitment were and are the face of grace in the midst of incredible self-sacrifice and service. Although she married into a traditional role of doctor's wife and homemaker, she never allowed that to limit who she perceived herself to be. Instead, she lived for her family and for her faith— and she defined her life for herself and celebrated it. She still does. And yes, she *is* amazing. Or my sister, whose grace is unmatched by anyone I've ever known. Her dedication, compassion and kindness never cease to amaze me.

Grace is a quality that women bring to every aspect of their lives: their quiet strength, in the face of the sometimes grinding monotony, is their steel; their compassion and faith, in the good times and the bad, are found in their everyday kindnesses; their words, their touch—a balm. A woman's everyday grace is the face of the Divine on Earth.

Every child grows up believing that he or she is invincible; identifying with heroes and heroines, essentially wanting to be a superhero. In fact, up until around age 10, most of us imagined ourselves to be just that, with all the accompanying secret powers and mysterious insights; all those things we "just knew" as children as we watched the world around us. In my day, there was Wonder Woman—with her island of fellow sisters, her golden amulets that defended her from dark forces, and her crazy, invisible flying machine, she had it all. There were other, more pedestrian role models to look to as well: Laura Ingalls Wilder from the Little House series, whose courage and independence were an inspiration; Judy Blume's Margaret, who gave voice to our insecurities about growing up; and Nancy Drew, whose methodical, studious habits and insatiable curiosity were preludes to who I and so many others of my generation became. We were also the inheritors of Title IX, legislation that demanded equal dollars be spent for girls' and women's sports as had been traditionally spent on boys. And trust me, growing up in Texas, that legislation made a big difference! These cultural icons from my generation, however, are small fry compared with today's plethora of women's sports idols, musicians, writers, artists, and activists. Girl Power is in. Riot Grrrls, post-feminist feminism, the womyn's movement—whatever the name, empowering women and girls is the new black. Fashion may finally be serving the interests of women, and it's about time! Young women now have more accessible and meaningful role models than at any other time in our modern culture. Aiming high is no longer unusual for women and girls.

As we grow up, however, most of us lose that sense of invincibility. Our personal power gets set aside for just getting along. Our identity as Infinity gets short-circuited, and we begin to seek outside ourselves for approval and acceptance. We begin to limit ourselves. Wanting to fit in, we make ourselves small. Authority figures question us, and we retreat. We begin to doubt ourselves instead of defending our truth. We second-guess our intuition—that core inner sense of knowing that had been with us (and is with us still, if we'd only listen)—and with it our connection to the One. We begin to question whether there ever really was a connection at all. Nature hates a vacuum, so in an effort to fill that space, that core need, that longing to belong, we sell ourselves short. Once belonging only to the Beloved, to God, we now abandon ourselves to whatever we can get. And in the getting, we lose the opportunity to receive what we truly need—our Self.

How do we reclaim our true identity, our connection to the One, our inner Self? First we must remember where it truly lies—in the one Creator, in being one with the Creator. When I was seven or eight years old, I woke up and thought to myself, "Something's missing." The loss was palpable. And in all the innocence and precociousness of my youth, I said to myself, "I'm going to spend the rest of my life trying to remember what I've forgotten." That was my moment of separation from the One. I have since spent many years consciously seeking what I had lost.

We all share this experience—the fall from grace. For some it's more traumatic; for others, there's no sense of loss at all, just an undifferentiated anxiety that something's not quite right or that something has gone terribly wrong. But just as we all share this experience of separation, we also share the potential to realize that oneness again. We all have the potential to experience our own human excellence and profound joy through the energy of the kundalini, the life force and excellence of the human psyche. This potent potential rests at the base of our spine and, when awakened, is the human expression of the Divine. As the kundalini rises, we experience bliss. We no longer call things good or bad, right or wrong; we simply acknowledge what is as being God and rejoice in the flow of life. As the kundalini returns, we are healed and our energy is restored. This is our birthright; this is grace.

In truth, these polarities—the childlike longing for superpowers and the adolescent-induced inferiority complexes—are simply the journey toward becoming a woman. Yet if you aren't careful, if you don't address them in consciousness and confront them head on, these attitudes can be carried into adulthood and grow more pronounced. The fantasies of superpowers grow into bloated, empty visions of grandiosity; adolescent insecurities grow into corrosive self-loathing. Instead, imagine taking that first step toward your true Self. Retire your superpowers to the shelf and drop your baggage at the curb; know that you are the wow, the juice, the life in every living thing—just by being you. Your creative spark, your limitless love, and your warmth and tenderness nurture every good thing into existence. You carry the hopes of the future even as you fulfill the needs of the present. Just be a woman—the Grace of God—because that is more than enough.

The desire to be bigger than life stems from our very nature as women. As women, we are infinitely creative, just as we are connected to the Infinite Creator. In the words of Yogi Bhajan, we are the "creativity of the Creator." This, of course, begs the question, What have we created?

Looking around at today's world, it would be easy to become discouraged; so much violence, poverty, ignorance, intolerance, and hatred—and so much of it at the expense of women. Are we the creators of this? Well, the short answer is yes. Our inability to forgive, our attachment to clan and kin, our jealousy and desire for more have wrought every kind of evil—war, murder, theft. The story of Adam and Eve has a kernel of truth in it, it's just interpreted incorrectly.

Let's say we accept as our premise that woman's desire and hubris led her astray—and man followed her. So, what's wrong with this traditional interpretation? The answer is the notion that it can't change! This notion is the fundamental mistake that misogynist cultures and religions have imposed on women for centuries; they have run with the idea of the woman's "fall" and used it to oppress her for generations. But woman is infinitely creative; her "fall from grace," if that's what we want to call it, can be corrected. She simply needs to embody her grace once again; then all paradise will be ours to enjoy once more.

So, how do you get "back to the garden"? Remember who you are—the Grace of God. Rejoice in the potent power of your infinite creativity. Women are the makers of the world—the creators, sustainers, and destroyers. This is the nature of God—G-O-D— generator, organizer, and deliverer. This is the nature of a woman, and her grace is the key to the transformation we seek, in the world and in ourselves. The graceful woman forgives, contains, molds, and generates her environments for peace and happiness—in her home, her community, and her world.

Grace Note

Take a moment. Close your eyes. Raise your arms above your head and feel as though you are encircling the entire universe in your arms. Experience your prayer supporting and containing the entire universe, your whole world. Feel your heart open. Breathe deeply and look within. You contain the entire universe within you. You are the cathedral, the temple, the mosque, the vaulted dome of the sky. You are the fathomless depths of the ocean; the quiet, gentle rain; and the wild, turbulent storm. You are the simple love song and the soaring choral anthem. Your quiet hum and sweet lullaby are the proverbial music of the spheres. Connect to the Infinite—here, in this moment. Remember who you are. Experience your vastness. Embrace your creativity. Embody your prayer. Then go and serve your environments with joy and grace.

The Adi Shakti

One of the most ancient symbols of the sacred feminine is the Adi Shakti. The oldest form of prayer, the Adi Shakti symbolizes the lone woman, her arms raised to the sky, curved in a graceful arc, as if holding the entire world and supplicating the universe to align itself with her word. This ancient symbol is the key to unlocking the power of our own sacred feminine. It reminds us of our infinity, our divinity.

The Adi Shakti represents the creative power that lies within every woman. And yet for her Shakti to be in balance, a woman must also relate to her Bhakti, her devotional nature. She must balance the polarities of the woman and the mother within her. Whether or not she ever has children of her own, every woman contains these two unique identities: the woman and the mother. "As a mother you are supposed to sacrifice, tolerate, be very patient, be very thoughtful of others, and understand all the pros and cons of any situation. As a woman you must give nothing; you have to protect yourself first; and you need not tolerate any nonsense. Woman must be able to ascertain which is the correct relationship—woman or mother," sword or shield.[2] Woman is the Shakti and Mother is the Bhakti; every woman must learn to apply these two distinct identities with skill and subtlety. This is her grace.

A woman's sword is her discerning nature, her capacity to see through to the root causes and motives in another and cut through them when necessary to protect herself or her family. A woman's sword is her word, her bluntness, her capacity to call a spade a spade, her inability to suffer fools. A woman's sword is her strength. Wielded wisely, she cultivates tolerance, prosperity, and peace. Used indiscriminately, she creates a great deal of damage. A woman's

2 © The Teachings of Yogi Bhajan, circa 1977

mothering nature—her shield—is nurturing, infinitely patient, and protective. She is the shield, devoting herself selflessly, to the point of sacrifice when necessary, to her children or her cause. Applied justly, a woman's mothering nature gives comfort and solace. Applied wrongly and she becomes a martyr, whose children loathe her and whose causes never receive the fruits of prosperity.

As a woman, you have the capacity to nurture everything into existence. You also have the capacity to destroy anything in your wake. Discerning when and how to apply Shakti or Bhakti means success or failure in your relationships, your goals, and even your destiny. Balancing these polarities is a woman's grace.

Woman & Infinity

Everything comes from the creativity of the woman—all the good and all the bad. Until a woman recognizes her shadow (the negative aspects of her nature) and understands its origin (her constant search for security), she'll continue to be ruled by it. A woman must accept her shadow, begin to manage it, and finally elevate herself above it. Otherwise, she'll react from ego or personal agenda, rather than respond from consciousness. In fact, much of the behavior that is perceived as negative in a woman comes from this need for security. The search for security—material, financial, or emotional—is completely natural; her very nature as a woman and a mother, both physically and psychologically, demands security. But it also makes her shortsighted. She loses her expansiveness, her connection to all that is. How can a woman maintain her grace and stay connected to her creativity, while at the same time trying to find the security she sorely needs, especially when the shadow side of her personality is so often triggered by insecurity? She must remember where her security truly lies—in Infinity.

Why do so many of us contract and control, when we could expand and excel? For one thing, we aren't taught to relate to our Infinity. From a very early age, we're taught to seek security from the approval of others. As young girls, the message we consistently receive has everything to do with making us smaller—feel smaller, act smaller, be smaller—and very little to do with helping us recognize how very *big* we actually are. In schools, girls are consistently called on less frequently than boys. Even in families, studies have shown that boys are given more attention. Around the world, especially in China and the Middle East, the mortality rate of girls is much greater than that of boys. Girls are routinely neglected, malnourished, and taken to the doctor much later than boys; so they often die of preventable diseases and conditions.

From a very early age, young women are taught to diminish themselves—to contract. Don't make trouble; be good. It reminds me of one of my favorite quotes from Laurel Thatcher Ulrich: "Well-behaved women rarely make history." In fact, many female figures in history are more notorious than notable—see Eve. In part, this is because history is written by men. It is also because the graceful, expansive identity of woman doesn't necessarily make the news, at least not for 20 years *or more* after the fact—see Mother Teresa.

The truth is, when you place your security in anything other than Infinity, you write your own recipe for misery, attachment, and depression. So, how do you begin to relate to your Infinity? First step: Don't feel small, act small, or be small. Don't contract; instead, expand and continue expanding. Second step: Experience yourself as the Infinity that you are. Marianne Williamson's poem "Our Deepest Fear"[3] has become famous because it calls on all of us to stop being small, to no longer be afraid of who we really are, to shine. This is the very definition of Adi Shakti—the primal power, the first light.

3 Williamson, Marianne, A Return to Love: *Reflections on the Principles of a Course in Miracles* (New York: Harper Collins, 1992).

"I am the light of my soul, I am bountiful, I am beautiful, I am bliss. I am, I am." This is the affirmation given to women by Yogi Bhajan that they might know their own true light; that they might know their own Divinity. What would it mean to be the light of our own souls? So often we hear people refer to "the light of my life," referring to their children or their spouses. But what if we each became the light of our own lives? How would that change us? How would it change our relationships?

As a single woman, I have no choice but to be the light of my own life; there's no one out there who can fill that void for me. But I think it's actually easier for me than for a woman who is in relationship to a husband and children. The very nature of her relationship leads her to extend outward, to serve and uplift. It's not too hard to see how that service can then become a role and eventually an identity. When that happens, a woman begins to perceive that the light is somehow outside herself; that the bounty, beauty, and bliss come from some outside source, rather than from within. This is the greatest tragedy that can happen to a woman. For in reality, everything comes from within her.

The world exists because of woman. Prosperity and bounty exist to decorate her. Men, women, and children all long to serve her, to be with her. Creativity and entrepreneurship exist because of her projection and her commitment to life and all living things. She is the bounty, the seed, and the harvest. Her energy, the moon, makes things grow. Her love and devotion allow everything within her influence to unfold. She is the cycle of life. She is the bliss, the nectar, the sweetness. She is the I am. With this affirmation—"I am, I am"—Yogi Bhajan references one of the oldest and most sublime literary definitions of God, the I am.[4] And in this way, woman recognizes herself as God, the co-creator of all that is.

4 Exodus 3:14: "And God said unto Moses, 'I am that I am.'"

May you recognize the Divine within you and may these pages awaken in you the art of being a woman. May you realize the everyday grace—the amazing grace—that you are in the lives of everyone you touch, each and every day. May you know yourself to be a woman, the Grace of God, and may that always be more than enough.

Chapter Two

Grace and the Art of Being

Woman is the axis of the entire creation. Why do flowers grow? So that men can pick them and bring them to you. Why does cotton grow? So that it can turn itself into cloth and be given to you as gifts. [5]

—*Yogi Bhajan*

The most challenging concept for a modern woman to accept—deep in her bones—is that she is a woman. As women, either we don't understand the inherent power of our identity, or if we do, we don't want to accept the responsibility that comes with that power. Meanwhile, the culture works to convince us that the only way to survive and thrive in today's world is to become men—but we aren't men! We're so much *more.*

5 © The Teachings of Yogi Bhajan, June 27, 1984

My name is Sat Purkh, which actually means True Being; it is my destiny name. That doesn't necessarily mean I "get it," but it does mean that I am challenged each and every day to fulfill that destiny—to be true, to rest in the identity of being, true being. I don't have to do anything, I simply have to be. Part of being true to my Self is being true to my identity as a woman, which isn't easy.

As women, we enter the world with our creativity fully present within us. Our ovaries contain all the eggs we will ever produce in our lifetime. We are born with the entire genetic code of our mothers, our ancestry within us, and this also contains our potential, our future. This fundamental creativity is our birthright; it is our security and our power. In many ways, the ovum, the egg, is a metaphor for the art of being a woman. The ovum settles into the tissue of the uterus, and it waits. It doesn't go out and seek anything. It simply glows; it is a radiant orb of potential life and light. It waits to be met, and it tests all that come. The sperm actually circle the ovum several times, as a kind of worship, before she allows one to penetrate and create union. It's the egg that chooses, not the sperm that conquers. How can this cellular story help us change our own stories of being a woman? Take a moment to let this reality sink in: You choose, from the deepest places within your being, at the cellular, vibratory level—you choose.

Men, on the other hand, have a radically different experience. In the womb itself, boys are subjected to a hormonal bath that, for all intents and purposes, cuts the communication between the two hemispheres of their brains, essentially leaving them "half-brained." To add insult to injury, infant boys enter the world without any creative, genetic material guaranteeing their future; that is, their sexual organs don't mature for several more years, so they are born without the inherent creativity that a girl child knows. Once the

Grace Note

Close your eyes. With your right hand on top of your left, palms up, bring the tips of your thumbs together, and relax your hands in your lap. Take a deep breath. Now imagine yourself as an orb of light—a pulsing, clear, shining body of light. Become completely still. Call out from your soul those things you long for. In your mind's eye, see them coming to you, orbiting you, longing to serve you.

Remain calm and still and relaxed. Let the breath come and go. Deeply meditate in this stillness, this light, this radiance that is you, that is woman. See your radiance expanding, enveloping the world and all its lively things. See yourself, worthy. And wait; wait patiently. Simply be and breathe deeply. In this way, all the world will come to serve you and your radiance.

cord is cut, they also lose that deep and profound connection with the mother. Whereas the girl child has the security of identity and creativity within her, boy children are completely dependent on the aura of the mother to maintain that nurturing connection and sense of self.

A girl child comes into the world fully aware of her creativity and secure in her identity. She has an innate sensibility and sensitivity to the Sacred, the Divine, the Infinite. She can call upon the Unknown as easily as breathing. She can know and relate to the inner Self without effort; it is her identity from the beginning. So, what happens? Why do we see so much insecurity, doubt, and self-deprecation in girls and young women? One answer could be that we are culturally conditioned to try to become a particular kind of beauty, to seek a certain level of approval and appreciation from others. This takes us out of our Self, our own unique qualities and gifts, making us vulnerable to the seeds of doubt and insecurity sown at an early age. A second answer could be that we are simply not informed. There's a fundamental misunderstanding of our bodies, as women, and how they really work.

Every woman has two arclines. An arcline is an energetic field that attracts, protects, and projects. One of these arclines, which we share with men, runs from ear to ear and is commonly depicted as a halo in religious paintings and artifacts. Women have a second arcline that runs from nipple to nipple across our Heart Center. These two arclines, combined with our aura, create an energy field that is sixteen times more sensitive, sixteen times more powerful, and sixteen times more intuitive than a man's. Because we live in a world of polarity, this same strength also has its costs: We are also more insecure, more neurotic, and more profoundly affected by what enters our arcline.

Here's an example: When a man and woman have sex, the man's aura is affected for 72 hours, at most; a woman's arcline at the Heart Center, however, is imprinted for 7 years! That's not a minor difference; that's a *world of difference*, and it comes from a woman's capacity to bear children. Her empathy, her compassion, and her innate ability to make connections with others all arise from her second arcline at the Heart Center. It's her gift. When combined with the arcline at the Brow Point, it gives her an incredible intuitive capacity to see the unseen and know the Unknown. But if the arcline—and how it functions—isn't respected, then it can also be a tremendous source of pain and heartache.

In the late 1960s and early 1970s, the sexual revolution told women that their sexuality was their own. The old taboos were thrown out for a newly found power and freedom in sexual expression. Of course, a woman has always intuitively known the power that her sex has over a man. Unfortunately, she has often used that power to get what she wanted. But even so, this power was always within a certain construct that still saw a woman as something to be protected, and even revered. By the time the late 1970s rolled around, an entire decade of women had marched in the streets in the name of empowerment and equal opportunity, even as they had thrown themselves to the dogs. No-fault divorce became the new normal, women no longer had any societal protections, and worst of all, they had fallen for the big lie—that being equal was better than being a woman.

How can we be equal to a man when we give birth to man? It's not possible. Yet we throw ourselves at the feet of the male-dominated culture and ask men to accept us, love us, honor us. Again, it's not possible. Women have earned equal protection under the law at great personal sacrifice, and those sacrifices must be honored. But we must also begin to assess the cost and reclaim the damages so that our daughters and granddaughters will not pay the same heavy price. We must learn to be women—graceful women—again.

To begin reclaiming our identity, we must accept, without reservation, what it means to be in a woman's body. We are sensitive. We are intuitive. We are creative. Our thoughts and actions have consequences that can stay with us for a lifetime. The bottom line is that we can get pregnant, and that possibility is in the back of every woman's mind for the better part of her adult life. Because of this ability, we think differently, we plan, we understand that there's a cost to everything.

It has taken me years to accept this truth about my Self and my body, to know that there's a cost to everything, especially sex. Trust me, I've tested it more than once and learned the hard way. For most of my 20s and early 30s, I approached my own sexuality with a recklessness that verged on self-destruction. This period in my life could easily be called "How to Have Sex Like a Man." Of course, at the time I believed I was just having a good time, being young, and enjoying my sexual freedom and the power I derived from it. There was a belligerence, an anger in me that played itself out through my sexuality. I resented that women were expected to play by a different set of rules. I resented that I was different, and that resentment was compounded by my frustration at not understanding why I was different. Although I had been raised in a tradition where sex before marriage was forbidden, I was never given a reason—and so I experimented.

I wanted to believe that I could have sex with impunity. Even now there are times when I still want to believe this! But I've learned that it is just not possible. Each time I engaged in intercourse with a man, my arcline was affected. And it's not only sex that affects our arcline. Exploitation, verbal abuse, sexual innuendo, and violence all negatively affect a woman and her arcline. What does that mean? Well, sexual intercourse can create a kind of "leak" in the energy field. Sexual relationships outside of commitment extend a woman's energy—and, like a rubber band that's been stretched too many times, after a while, that energy can't rebound. It loses its elasticity. Our radiance is weakened; our boundaries aren't as strong; and we're rendered more vulnerable, insecure, and instable. If, on the other hand, we respect the natural boundaries that accompany our arclines, we become invincible. Nothing can penetrate us or throw us off balance; we contain and cover everything and everyone in our lives; we are courageous, boundless, and prosperous.

As women, we must become the conscious caretakers of our bodies, our psyches, and our aura. We must begin to utilize our arclines to positively project and manifest our lives as we want them to be. We must begin to look to Infinity for our security and meditate on our own creative capacity. We must drop any notion of searching, grasping, or extending ourselves to get what we need. Instead, we must return to our essential nature—the infinite creative potential—and sit, meditate, and relax. Every good thing will come to us if we allow it. This is grace.

Women are amplifiers. Our nature is to nurture, to bring to fruition any seed, any thought, any idea. The combination of the arcline at the Brow Point and the arcline at the Heart Center gives us a unique capacity to not only beam and project through the Third Eye, but also nurture and nurse that projection through our prayer at the Heart Center. With our beaming, projective capacity we can create our world, our environments, and our lives in any way we like. So why not create peaceful, cozy environments filled with mutual respect, kindness, and compassion? Imagine if each one of us used our creative capacity in this way? Imagine a world at peace. This is our grace—a woman's grace.

Being Beautiful

Our two arclines and our aura, which are the keys to our intuitive, sensitive, and projective powers, also generate our radiance, which

---

Grace Note

Tune In. Close your eyes. Rest your hands on your knees, palms up, with your thumb and index fingertips touching. Begin to drink the breath in a single, deep, long sip through a rounded mouth. Exhale through your nose slowly. Take several long deep breaths in this way; sipping the breath through the mouth and exhaling through the nose. Then inhale, suspend the breath, and meditate on zero: "All is zero; I am zero; each thought is zero; my pain is zero; every problem is zero; any illness is zero." Bring into your awareness every negative emotion, thought, habit, and pattern. As each negative thought crosses your mind, bring it to zero—make it into a single point of light, growing smaller and smaller, until it becomes zero. Exhale and repeat, breathing in a comfortable rhythm. Repeat this until every negative thought has become zero. Now meditate on what you most need. What quality or condition do you most desire for your complete happiness and personal growth? Find a single word, such as "Prosperity," "Health," "Relationship," "Guidance," "Knowledge," "Luck," and lock in on that word. Visualize the different facets of it. Form a complete picture of what this would look like in your own life. Now inhale and hold the breath as you beam that thought— that single word and your vision of it—in a continuous stream from your Brow Point. Exhale and relax. Inhale and beam out from your Brow Point that which you most need to fulfill your life. Exhale and relax. Continue in this way until you feel a natural smile come to your face. Congratulations!

---

is the key to true beauty. We live in a culture that constantly puts pressure on us to conform to a certain standard of beauty. This standard is completely unrealistic; but more than that, it's not authentic—it's not you. This notion of "beauty" doesn't serve our identity or our long-term health and vitality. And if you've ever had even the slightest cold, much less a severe, chronic health condition,

You've created the emotional and mental environments that make it possible for everything you need to come to you. Now, to seal the practice, inhale and move the shoulders, arms and spine. Then stretch the arms up, spread the fingers wide, and breathe deeply a few times.[1]

1 From the meditation, *Beaming and Creating the Future,* © The Teachings of Yogi Bhajan, June 12, 1990.

you know that beauty cannot exist without the foundation of vibrant health and a sense of well-being—an inner identity.

If beauty is simply our radiance from within projecting out, how do we let that inner light shine? How do we stoke our inner fire? How do we cultivate our radiance? An essential ingredient is acceptance; accepting ourselves exactly as we are, good and all. Our culture wants us trimmed and clipped like a well-kept lawn, but we're not manufactured, manicured mannequins. We're women! We're the embodiment of the Divine. Every hair has a purpose. Every curve is a blessing, an expression of our creative, feminine power. To deeply relax into the body, as it is, to accept and bless every hair, every mole, every freckle, every fold as exactly as it should be is to embody our femininity. It's the first step to true beauty.

The hair on our legs serves to balance and stimulate the lower triangle—our lower back, sex organs, and digestive tract. The hair under our arms stimulates the lymphatic system in our breasts and along the outer ribcage, supporting the detoxification of fatty tissues in the breasts and helping to clear the waste generated from the lungs. Growing the hair on our crown to its natural length supports the protein balance in the tissues and extends our aura. Hair is an energy antenna; when grown to its full length, it draws in the solar energy at the crown of the head and increases our radiant body's projection—up to 9 feet! Grow your hair—everywhere— and experience what it's like to completely and deeply accept your body exactly as it is—as Mother Nature made it.

I grew up in the South, where it was common to hear the women of my mother's generation say, "Let me go put my face on." I was fortunate in that my own mother was, for the most part, immune to the pressures of Southern belle society. She was a tomboy from northern California who didn't start wearing makeup until she was in her 50s! That's not to say she didn't exert other pressures on herself, along with my sister and I, to fit the "beauty ideal"—she did. But makeup, thankfully, wasn't one of them. The cosmetic and beauty industry (skin and hair care; fragrance) brings in billions of dollars a year on the backs of women and their insecurities. Now, there's nothing fundamentally right or wrong about wearing makeup or not wearing makeup; everything is a play. But if you're going to buy into it, know what you're buying into: an industry that exploits women, young and old; that plays on their fears, from acne to aging; and that exacts an impossible—air-brushed—standard of beauty. Is that really a reflection of you?

The new fashion statement is to be photographed without makeup. It's a sign of courage, bravery even, for a woman, especially one in the public eye. Magazines and talk shows feature women in their natural state as an exercise in empowerment; yet somehow those women never seem that empowered. When we can turn that around and empower women everywhere to simply be themselves, to stand before the mirror and like what they see, we'll have won a great victory. And then the play can be just that—play; not the daily, grinding exploitation of women's fears and growing girls' insecurities about their bodies.

The Path to Inner Beauty

A woman's path to inner beauty involves several habits that, if applied daily, will give her the key to true radiance—that inner light that can never be put out.

Hydrotherapy. In ancient Ayurvedic practice, hydrotherapy—cold showers—is known as *ishnan.* Cold showers? I know! Trust me, I know. But if you want the quickest way to truly vibrant health, vitality, and longevity, this is it. Cold showers are invigorating; they flush out the capillary beds at the surface of the skin and bring renewed blood and oxygen deep into the organs and tissues. Forget about all those expensive creams and skin tonics; a cold shower does more to rejuvenate the skin than anything else.

Before you say "No way!" here are a few other benefits to persuade you to give cold showers a try:

- They strengthen the parasympathetic and sympathetic nervous systems.

- They contract the muscles and cause them to eliminate toxins and poisons more quickly.

- They bring the power of resistance and resilience to the body.

- They strengthen the mucous membranes.

- They prevent the body from developing an extra layer of fat, which is good for the liver.

- They balance all the glands.

- They help prevent circulatory problems and neuralgia.

Before you try taking your first cold shower, however, you should know a few things. Don't practice cold shower therapy when you're on your menstrual cycle. Also, don't just get in and suffer! There's a simple way to approach a cold shower that not only makes it more palatable but also serves to enrich your skin even more. Begin with a massage of almond, sesame, or olive oil; almond has the most neutral scent and is also the most compatible to the skin's natural emollients. Use long, vigorous strokes on your limbs and circular strokes on your joints. Be sure to massage your breasts, too. After the massage, step into the shower. Let the cold water strike your body while you briskly massage the water into your skin. Move! Chant! Call on God! Let out that great Yawp!

Don't stand under the water the entire time. Instead, rub your skin vigorously under the cold spray, then step out of the shower and continue to massage your skin. Then step back in. Allow your breasts, belly, and underarms to be massaged by the water; massage your entire body with your hands. But keep the outside of your hips away from the direct stream of cold water, or wear a towel to cover your hips and thighs. This protects the femur from sudden changes in temperature. (The femur regulates the production of calcium in the body and is very sensitive to temperature.)

Repeat this process three or four times until you feel warm, even though the water is still cold. At this point, your capillaries have opened up, bringing blood to the skin's surface, making you feel warm. When you're finished, dry yourself briskly with a towel. Of course, the ideal is a daily cold shower; but once a week is a good start. And if you have to take a warm shower, take it *after* your cold shower. Whatever you do, don't take a *hot* shower—nothing ages you faster.

Breathing the Body Beautiful. The breath of life is just that—life. The quality of life you have, or can have, largely depends on the quality of your breath. There are so many different breath techniques, or pranayams, but one in particular—the One Minute Breath—develops a woman's Radiant Body. When mastered, this breath cultivates a deep, penetrating, pervasive peace in the body and the psyche. It expands the consciousness in a way that allows for unlimited patience and equanimity. You can defeat anything with this breath. It opens up your intuition; reduces anxiety, fear, and worry; and allows you to use your entire brain—both hemispheres—to maximize your potential.

The practice of this breath should be taken slowly. Don't expect to master it the first few times you try it. Instead, build a relationship with this breath so that you can begin to master it not only on your meditation cushion but also in your office or the driver's seat or on line at the grocery. Start slowly: Inhale 8 seconds, suspend 8 seconds, exhale 8 seconds. From there, slowly build up to the complete one-minute ratio: inhale 20 seconds, suspend 20 seconds, exhale 20 seconds.

The suspension of the breath can be challenging for beginners; the key is finding the right balance of relaxation and engagement of the muscles. When you suspend the breath in, there shouldn't be any sense of constriction or tightness in your ribs, belly, or face. Instead, lift your collarbones slightly, engage the navel point gently, and relax your shoulders. In this way, the suspended breath becomes a gateway to *shuniya*—the zero point, a place of profound quiet and stillness. The exhale and the inhale are smooth and slow. This technique takes a while to master. Don't force it; instead, keep relaxing into the breath. Still your mind; still your thoughts; slow down and don't grasp for anything—especially not the breath. In this way, your Radiant Body will become bright, tipped with gold and silver, and you will naturally attract everything you need into your life, without lifting a finger.

You can start with as little as 3 minutes a day (three deep breaths) and increase your practice over time, up to 31 or even 62 minutes a day. In addition to the One Minute Breath, there is a simple exercise set, *Keeping the Body Beautiful*, which helps maintain your radiance, incorporates the deep breath, and includes an exercise that Yogi Bhajan said was the "test" of a woman. Work to master your breath so that you can master your mind. Work to maintain a standard of flexibility in your spine, so that you can be as flexible as you need to be in your life! This simple series of exercises takes less than 10 minutes, and it's a great way to build up your radiance, strength, and flexibility to face the day ahead.[6]

You Really Are What You Eat. That old adage from our childhood is absolutely true. There are so many great resources out there now for making positive changes in one's diet (for more on this topic, see Chapter Eight). But what parts of your diet can actually change your *face*, your *grace*, *your radiance?* The primary culprit, as illustrated by Yogi Bhajan, is sugar:

> *Fructose, sucrose, whatever you want to call it, is the enemy of a woman's youth. When I see you eating cake, ice cream, cookies, and chocolate this and chocolate that, and then you say, "No, no, it's honey, not sugar," it doesn't bother me. But I know that the shine in you, the shine of a woman, is going to be lost. There is only one enemy of the woman—and that is sweetness in any shape or form. I know you don't want to hear it, but it makes you look old. That glow, which a woman produces because of her hormones, is gone.*
>
> *Watch how politely you are hooked to sugar. Watch very clearly and understand it. Go for one week on a diet free of all sorts of sugar. Notice the change; you will be shocked. Simply understand that there are certain things that don't suit you.*[7]

The second precaution every woman must take toward food is that it must clear the body within 18 to 24 hours of eating. Most Americans are constipated and don't know it. Ideally your bowels should move each time you eat. That's three times a day! Strangely enough, this fact is a shock to most people, even those in the health professions. But at minimum, for good health and radiance, you should move your bowels once a day—first thing in the morning.

6 © The Teachings of Yogi Bhajan, October 1969. See the appendix for a complete write-up of this and other Kundalini Yoga exercises.
7 © The Teachings of Yogi Bhajan, Circa 1983

Our systems change over time. What we could eat as teenagers simply won't pass this test; instead, we walk around feeling bloated, heavy, and congested when we eat too many processed foods, cheese, or white flour, not to mention the density of meat or the heavy metals in fish. Sometimes, simply eating too late can give us indigestion and heartburn. Women's systems are so sensitive that Yogi Bhajan recommended an eating regimen that allows for the greatest assimilation and digestion, while also helping women maintain their weight and their "lightness of being"—their inner glow. Start light—a breakfast drink (green drink or protein drink) or fruit and plain yogurt; follow this with one large meal at midday, an afternoon snack of fruit or another energy drink, and then fasting after 4 p.m. or a light meal of steamed greens and rice or a vegetable broth soup. In this way, your body moves through the day with everything it needs, while remaining light and focused on the tasks at hand, instead of struggling to digest the indigestible.

One final note about food and the ways in which we eat—or don't eat: In a culture obsessed with weight and body image, food, which should be nourishing and fulfilling, often becomes a blight. Food is so rooted in our notion of security, love, and family that it can become really twisted. I have lots of issues around food, as most women do. In my own family, we range from emotional eaters to binge eating to anorexia to every other disorder you can name. It's been painful to witness these struggles in myself and in others in my family, but it's also been a revelation. Our issues with food are often the deepest, most intimate barriers we experience to the Self—our True Being. Yet, depending on the extremity of the disorder, these intimate issues are played out in public, whether through obesity or in starving oneself to death. This dance between the private behaviors and the public witness to their consequences makes the relationship to food and the recovery from food issues all the more challenging. So, as much as we may know what to do and how to do it, for most of us, the relationship to food is the most challenging and profound change we will ever make in our lives. I know for myself that it is still a work in progress. So, be kind to yourself. Make one change at a time. Understand that you may have to start over again, and again, and again. Be patient. Savor your food and savor your Self. This is grace.

Walk This Way. Finally, take yourself for a walk. The best thing a woman can do for herself each day is walk. It's the perfect exercise. The human body was built to walk—and to walk long distances. Walking up to 5 miles a day keeps a woman's pelvis and spine flexible, in alignment, and moving freely and without pain. Her digestion is stimulated as well, strengthening and toning the large muscles and keeping her overall metabolism in tune. Walking, when combined with regulated breathing techniques, can be an extraordinary daily practice.[8]

Grace Note

Try this simple technique to invigorate your next walk. For four steps, sniff a little bit of air through the nose with each step (also known as segmented breath); then exhale in one long stroke, equaling four steps. Four counts in, with segmented breath; and four counts out, in one long exhale. This type of breathing will oxidize the bloodstream and energize every cell of your body.

8 See Breathwalk® by Yogi Bhajan and Gurucharan Singh Khalsa (New York: Broadway Books, 2000)

Walking also gives a woman's creativity a little breathing room—room to roam, to stretch herself beyond the usual everyday activities, thoughts, and worries, and to expand into freedom. So much of our life is spent running around in circles upon circles of errands, deliveries, carpools, ball games, shopping, and more. To put our feet on the ground and connect once again to our bodies and our breath, to the earth and the sky, is priceless. One of my favorite books, *If You Want to Write* by Brenda Ueland, speaks to the benefits of walking and the creative process. No destination, no exits, just putting one foot in front of the other and seeing where curiosity and circumstance lead. Here in the Southwest, it's very healing to set out into the arroyos, with the wide-open sky above and the rock formations shadowed against the backdrop of the Sangre de Cristo mountains. No particular path, just following wherever the eye may lead. It's also great fun to set out in the city— New York, Seattle, Chicago—allowing your intuition to guide you. At each corner, ask yourself, Which way am I called to turn? You may run into something beautiful—you may run into You.

The art of being and being beautiful are one and the same. A woman, by definition, is beauty. She is the creative potential of the Infinite. Her grace is her face. Look into the mirror and see beauty—before you and within you—and simply be. This is the art of being. This is your grace.

Grace Note

Here's another beautiful, simple practice to connect you and your breath to the beauty available to you with every step you take. Before you head out the door, take a moment to meditate on this simple prayer. Read through it three to five times; then close your eyes, inhale deeply, and tune in to yourself and the beauty within you. Open your eyes, inhale deeply, and head out the door, breathing in the beauty all around you.

In beauty I walk
With beauty before me I walk
With beauty behind me I walk
With beauty above me I walk
With beauty below me I walk
With beauty about me I walk
It is finished in beauty
It is finished in beauty

~Traditional Navajo Prayer

Take this prayer with you throughout your day, every step of the way.

Chapter Three

The Art of Sexuality

Maintaining Your Grace

Never try to be too sweet that everybody eats you; never try to be too bitter that everybody throws you away. Be just right. If you ever asked me how to live like God, I would tell you to live in grace. Live in your grace.[9]

—*Yogi Bhajan*

Kundalini Yoga as taught by Yogi Bhajan® is juicy; it's sexy. Throughout my years of searching for a path that would allow me to express my entire nature, my entire being, I had tried just about everything: Native American sweat lodge ceremonies and medicine circles; both Tibetan and Zen Buddhism; Creation Spirituality in the context of progressive, reformed Christianity; Hatha Yoga and

9 © The Teachings of Yogi Bhajan, July 14, 1975

Hindu mantra practices; Sufi mysticism; and more. Each added to my understanding of myself, but none seemed to encompass my entire being. All of them asked me to set aside a part of myself in one way or another. Then I found Kundalini Yoga as taught by Yogi Bhajan®, and I realized I'd found a path that allowed for the human experience: the good, the bad, and the ugly, as well as the ecstatic, the juicy, and the sublime.

Kundalini Yoga as taught by Yogi Bhajan® is a householder path. What does that mean? Well, it means we marry and have families and jobs and responsibilities out in the world, even as we practice the yogic disciplines. It means we have sex—really good sex! Yogi Bhajan's primary complaint when he came to the West (besides discovering that women were being called "chicks") was that women weren't trained to express their sexuality in a healthy way. He arrived here at the height of the social revolutions of 1969: the anti-war movement, the sexual revolution, and women's rights. At the time, even though women believed they were free, he saw only drug addiction, slavery to impulse, and exploitation of women under the guise of liberation. The 1970s proved his vision to be true. How could it have all gone so wrong? And how can we begin to make it right?

Let's start with what went wrong. A lot of post-feminists out there claim that feminism failed to meet its goals, including equal pay for equal work, among others (though with the passing of the Lilly Ledbetter Fair Pay Act in 2009, that final hurdle was passed). In the pursuit of equality, women failed themselves in many ways. They lost something unique to their own identity as women—their grace, their femininity. And although women have moved beyond the backlash of the 1980s and 1990s, there is still a sense that somehow, somewhere, something went terribly awry. How did the conversation about freedom and equality get so contorted, so twisted?

Much of this conversation is rooted in deep-seated conditioning, which transcends any one culture and lies at the heart of how men and women are perceived, both sexually and in our traditional and not-so-traditional gender roles. Sensuality and manipulation are hallmarks of how women are often perceived throughout the world, which is one reason so many cultures have suppressed women, including their bodies, their reproductive rights, and their prosperity.

The first thing that we as women must understand is the power that our sexuality and our creativity wield over men. We create men—they come from our wombs, they nurse at our breasts, they turn to us for comfort as children and as men; they are built to seek us out, to desire us, merge with us, even conquer us. In effect, a man's life revolves entirely around women. As we've seen, it's impossible for men and women to be equal. In fact, in our search for equality, we have actually been diminishing ourselves. Until we accept the difference between men and women, as well as the power and responsibility that accompany that difference, we will never be able to shift the conversation back to the ideals we all long for—mutually supportive, loving, gracious families and the peaceful coexistence of peoples all around the world.

Don't get me wrong, equality under the law was hard-fought for, and even today it is still regularly tested. The fight has been worth it, because with it has come some beneficial changes in our culture. However, some of the fruits of that fight didn't turn out so great. Sexual liberation, for example, has become just one more way for women to be exploited—but this time we did it to ourselves! Once viewed as the property of men, women are now often viewed as being either respectable because of their positions as wife and daughter or not so respectable because of a more open exchange like prostitution In either case, property is still property. Only now, women have the "liberty" to give themselves away. The heartache that has come from this fundamental breakdown in a woman's worth is hard to factor or account for; but needless to say, generations of women have been sacrificed to this lie.

From Girls to Women

The idea of the graceful, noble women—the queen—has been degraded to such an extent that it sometimes feels like the last few vestiges of powerful women lie in the "queens" of the hip-hop world: Queen Latifah and Alicia Keys, to name a couple. Instead, the perverted notion of the madonna/whore polarity, which Madonna so brilliantly capitalized on throughout the 1980s and 1990s, now seems to reign as the primary projection of the woman in the West. Girls are being pressured to grow up faster and faster. The sexualization of young girls is seen in fashion trends, TV and print ads, and movie trailers, as well as in the news—and it's only growing worse. Girls as young as 5 and 6 are dressed in clothes appropriate to a woman in her 20s.

Girls are no longer allowed to be girls; the consciousness of their bodies and their sexuality is imposed on them at an earlier age than ever before. I'll never forget my shock at seeing my 13-year-old niece wearing thong underwear—really? And she's from a conservative family! Imagine the struggle for identity that young girls face when raised in families where they're *encouraged* to "be sexy"—it's even modeled for them by their mothers! Very little innocence remains in the West; modesty is mocked and belittled, seen as provincial and old-fashioned. And those cultures in the East that still uphold an ideal of the graceful woman are, unfortunately, the greatest culprits of repressive and oppressive treatment of women and girls. In fact, these cultures often display the greatest hypocrisy in regard to women: While they worship the goddess and revere their middle-class women as wives and mothers, they sell poorer girls into sexual slavery—and they see no problem with this inherent contradiction and incredible injustice.

It's challenging for me, as a Western woman, to talk about notions of modesty and responsibility without hearing the voice in the back of my head saying, "It's not our fault that men sexualize everything about us!" And in a sense, this is true. In cultures where women dress very modestly, the exposure of just an ankle becomes the source of heated debate. This is, of course, ridiculous and becomes the counterargument for "Let it all hang out," which is equally untenable. So we must find a tempered approach to the notion of grace and the identity of women as sexual beings.

How do we find that balance? The Teachings of Yogi Bhajan empower a woman not only to seek that balance but also to find it, live it, and teach it to others. She is radiant, noble, courageous, and strong. She is graceful, kind, and compassionate. She is "strong as steel, steady as stone."[10] She is the embodiment of the divine. And as that embodiment, she is sexual. But this sexuality is rooted in creativity, consciousness, and delight—even ecstasy. This sexuality is a path to her awakening, not an obstacle. Her grace is her strength, not her weakness.

Here's my own story of transformation: I grew up in a conservative Christian home. Wearing shorts after the age of 11 or 12 wasn't allowed, which was challenging for the tomboy that I was. Although I found it unfair at the time, there was a part of my consciousness that understood, even at that young age, the reason my family

10 Livtar Singh, "Song of the Khalsa"

Grace Note

Sit quietly. Inhale deeply, exhale completely, and see yourself as the 10-year-old girl you once were. Feel the play of the sun on your skin, run through the field of your imagination, and remember your innocence; recall your curiosity. What was your first awakening, the realization of your own burgeoning sexuality? Inhale deeply, place your hands at your heart, and bow to your 10-year old self—acknowledge her experience; then exhale.

Continue to sit quietly. Inhale deeply and recall your first kiss. Perhaps it was a game as a child or at the neighbor's pool party or during a school field trip. Was it shocking? Was it sweet? Was it frightening? Recall the experience and breathe. Embody this memory—and that girl—with the woman you are now. What is your experience in your body, now, as you recall this memory? Inhale deeply, place your hands at your heart, and bow to your experience; feel it, and with the exhale, release it.

Continue to sit quietly. Inhale deeply and with the breath, use your imagination to merge your identity now with the 10-year-old girl you once were. Allow these two identities to inform the other. Merge strength with innocence; allow wonder and curiosity to inform cynicism. Experience your radiance. Now, in your mind's eye, walk out into the world. Take yourself through an entire day and visualize—project—how the world sees you. Notice and observe its respect; see its reverence. Breathe it in. Inhale deeply, place your hands at your heart, and bow to yourself. Exhale with a smile. This is your grace.

expected me to dress differently from my peers. I went on to become a fairly vocal feminist—in fact, I still am—sexually active and in full possession of my power as a woman. And as much as I thrilled in the early expression of that power, it soon grew old. It quit working. I wasn't getting what I wanted—whether that want was through conditioning or true longing, I'll never know. In either case, the cozy, intimate, committed relationship wasn't materializing. I was never very feminine, but using my power through sex wasn't working either.

I started studying Kundalini Yoga as taught by Yogi Bhajan®. I processed a lot of grief in the early years of my practice, until I came to a point of understanding: My purity existed beyond anything I had done or would do. It was self-existent; it was within me; it was me—despite my past or my future. This was tremendously empowering to me. I experienced a profound renewal. This doesn't mean I was by any measure "perfect" from then on; but I was working toward an identity that could encompass all of me, an identity that could express my power in a way that maintained my own grace, my own divinity.

Throughout this process, I was continually challenged to revisit the way I presented myself to the world. I began to understand that the clothing I selected was my projection. In the beginning, I was completely blind to the effect my dress may or may not have had; but over time, I came to realize the power of projection, and I became much more discriminating in what I wore. Modesty, which had always been somewhat the "norm" for me because of my upbringing, became a more conscious and mindful pursuit.

Cut to the present. I am now a woman who wears a turban *and* a *chuni*, which is basically a sheer scarf draped over my head and across my neck and shoulders. I wear it because it's a technology that supports my grace, cultivates my femininity, and reminds me of my identity. It supports the arcline; it projects a grace that my own personality still hasn't quite managed to manifest; and it reminds me to be gentle, with myself and with others. The response that it provokes in the wider world is always fascinating to witness: from curiosity and fascination to judgment and condescension. The response within myself has also been interesting to witness: One day I feel beautiful, graceful, and radiant, and the next I feel like it might choke me! I have finally come to a point where I have noticed a marked difference in how I experience my day if I forget to wear it—and it's not a pleasant difference. I'm harsher, more emotionally volatile, easily irritated, quick to anger, and prone to outbursts. Beyond these contrasting reactions to this particular way of presenting myself, I can say this about my overall experience: The chuni provides a tremendous buffer for me as a single woman in a world that is still primarily characterized as "a man's world." No man has ever whistled at me, disrespected me, or spoken harshly to me when I'm wearing my chuni. Try it; you may just find you like it!

Sexual Expression & the Graceful Woman

Returning to Yogi Bhajan's initial shock at the lack of education around sexuality and sexual expression, let's move into the technology of intimacy and intercourse. I can't speak for how sex education is addressed internationally, other than the obvious lack of education around family planning, HIV, and mutual consent. But here in the United States, sex education is either an impotent cry for abstinence or a dry wasteland of facts and statistics entirely dedicated to terrifying young men and women about pregnancy. Granted, I don't necessarily want public schools teaching about intimacy, individuation, and sexual expression, but unfortunately, it's not happening in the home either.

My family was the rare exception, I think. Unusually open about discussing sex, my first "sex talk" was when I was 10 years old. My mom and dad sat me down to talk about boys. It was a cautionary tale, letting me know what *not* to do. It was also my first lesson in understanding my responsibility around sex and my interactions with boys—and men. My dad explained that if I touched a boy in a certain way, I created what was, for all intents and purposes, an uncontrollable reaction in a young man's body. At age 10, this information felt a bit foreign and strange—and of course, it didn't include any of the nuances that concern true intimacy with a young man nor the frame of self-worth and self-respect that would have benefitted me as a young woman; but it was a beginning. And because of that beginning, I was always comfortable asking my parents anything concerning sex.

At the same time, I was still being presented with mixed messages. Growing up in a conservative home where sex was prohibited before marriage, I was nevertheless encouraged to be attractive, "sexy," so that boys, and then men, would be interested in me. Marriage was the goal, the driving narrative of my life, and any expression of sexuality outside that narrative was deemed "bad," immoral even. This became a devastating narrative for me personally, because marriage, it seemed, just wasn't in the cards, and my inability to "land" a man became a source of shame. The pursuit of that unrealized goal was the fruit of a lot of suffering and self-destructive behavior. I was never given the permission—or the tools—to simply be myself, to be with my Self, which is a woman's grace.

Because young girls' bodies are sexually maturing at younger and younger ages, there's tremendous social and physiological pressure (don't underestimate the power of hormones!) to act on that sexual identity. But their physical maturity is in no way a reflection of their emotional or mental readiness to be sexual beings. Yogi Bhajan advised young men and women to wait until they were 25 to engage in sexual behavior; in this way, they have the time and space and opportunity to form an identity free from the tremendous pressure that sex and sexual behavior imposes.

How does a young woman maintain her grace as she explores the nature of her sexuality? How does she connect to the juice without having "juicy" written across the seat of her pants, which, incredibly, is in style today! It's critical for a young woman to connect to her own being first—her identity—and then begin to explore her sexuality within herself. To know her own body. To learn what pleases her, explore her own physiology, and mine the depths of her own sensuality—all in the privacy of an experience with herself. A woman's first orgasm should ideally be with herself. Yogi Bhajan called a woman's exploration of her own sexuality— and her climax—*tiding*. It's a beautiful metaphor for the sensuous nature that is a woman's body—the sea—and the overwhelming ecstasy that is that seventh wave, the tiding experience.

When I was 23, I was living in a co-op in Southern California. It seemed that we had all been born in the wrong decade; each of us throwbacks to an earlier, more permissive era. That permissiveness created a really safe place for me to explore my sexuality. I had had sexual encounters in college but had still never experienced my own orgasm—and I was longing to learn how to please myself, so that my encounters with men would be more fulfilling. It was a frustrating enterprise, to say the least: long conversations with my roommate, who gave me tips and shared her experience; weekends of trial and error; and then, ahhhh! I was finally able to relax enough to submerge into the rolling wave that is tiding. The beauty of this experience, within this environment, was that the entire household celebrated with me: My roommate went out and bought a cake, and we all celebrated my awakening together! Those were the days, as they say. But most women don't have that kind of supportive environment in which to explore their bodies and their sexuality. Hence, the number of women who never achieve orgasm in their adult lives remains higher than one would imagine.

The Secrets to Sexual Satisfaction

As women, we are responsible for our sexual experience. It obviously helps to have a willing and eager partner. But still, in the end, we must know our bodies well enough to understand what sexual positions will most likely lead to our own orgasm, so that we can set ourselves up for a successful, fulfilling, intimate experience. There are two primary relationships that come into play here: the distance between a woman's vagina and her clitoris and the position of the vagina itself. The vagina has three primary positions: upper, lower, and normal. Like Goldilocks and the three bears, this represents three primary categories: too hot, too cold, and just right.

Thirty percent of women have a vagina that is in an upper position, which means their clitoris is very close to the vaginal opening. When combined with a clitoris that is on the pons, these women climax very easily and with very little stimulation. If anything, their sexual proclivity is an obstacle to a man's potential pleasure because of their easy and early orgasm, which doesn't provide the necessary friction—the "grab"—that's needed for the male orgasm.

The majority of women—60 percent—have a lower vaginal opening, which means the distance ratio to the clitoris is much larger. In this position, a woman must be stimulated manually in order to have an orgasm. To feel satisfied, it's recommended that she orgasm three times prior to intercourse and an additional three or four times post-coitus. She can self-stimulate or her partner can, but it *must* be done—so, get to work ladies! This lower position also requires deep penetration, usually from behind, and lots of manual stimulation in order to achieve orgasm. A woman with this physiology climaxes more easily if she is on top. Two other positions also facilitate orgasm: if she has several pillows placed beneath her pelvis when on her back, or if her legs are over the shoulders of her partner. Because the majority of women fall into this category, you can easily see why so many women express frustration in their sexual experiences, especially if they are unaware of the amount of stimulation necessary for their satisfaction or if they are uncomfortable asking for what they need.

The final category is what is called "normal," even though only about 10 percent of women are built this way. Here, the clitoris is "just right"—just above the vagina—so that with the right stimulation, orgasm is achieved in any position and in concert with your partner.

What does all this mean? It means you need to explore your body and know what works for you, so that when you are in an intimate, committed relationship, you can experience that merger with your partner that builds the relationship, rather than experiencing the frustration that often comes with unfulfilled desires and poor communication. Your partner will be grateful.

The other common problem with sexual expression is that we don't allow enough time. Yogi Bhajan cautioned that "if you don't have at least an hour to devote to the sexual encounter, then just give each other a foot rub and go to sleep." The difference between a woman's orgasm and a man's is so profound that it takes patience and a sophisticated sense of timing in order for each person to feel satisfied. When Yogi Bhajan first came here, he described what he was observing—better known today as a "quickie" or a "hook up"—as "sandwich sex," implying that packaged between a hello and a goodbye were 3 minutes that left you unsatisfied and with no small case of indigestion. Instead, the sexual experience between committed partners should be a moveable feast, a delight that begins 72 hours ahead of time, in the living room or the kitchen, with a small gesture, a light touch, a kind word; each person relishing in the delight to come, looking forward to it with no small measure of anticipation.

As a woman, take the time you need to prepare yourself. Remember, you are responsible for your own experience. When the day arrives, give yourself some time to take a relaxing bath; wash your hair; oil and perfume your body; prepare the bedroom with incense, candles, flower petals, clean sheets—whatever makes you feel beautiful and sensuous and allows you to delight in the space and the experience. Relax. Then proceed slowly, deliberately, methodically toward your own and your partner's complete satisfaction. There is an order, a prescription of sorts, that leads to a woman's satisfaction sexually— and both men and women need to be trained in it.

First, a woman's breasts must be stimulated, caressed, squeezed, pinched; second, the neck—stroke, nibble, and caress; third, the lips—kiss, bite, and lick; fourth is the cheeks; fifth is the ears, a most sensitive area. After the ears, remember the spine. The thighs are seven, a good squeeze and a bite on the hamstring is both a delight and a shock; the calves, eight; and the clitoris or vagina, nine. As Yogi Bhajan said, "If you use any other order, you are an idiot. Furthermore, this act must not take less than 30 minutes to an hour. Within that time, playing with that kind of energy, in this area, and in this order, your woman will have the 7 to 9 foot aura that you need."[11] This entire procedure fills the arcline with energy and creates the radiance a man needs in order to experience satisfaction and not be "drained" after the sexual encounter. How

---

11 From "The Secret to Sexual Satisfaction," in *Man to Man* (Santa Cruz, NM: Kundalini Research Institute, 2008)

will you know that it's working? Well, your partner should have a few bite marks and scratches to show for his efforts. And with that in mind, we all may need to try a little harder!

For a woman, what happens after sex is just as important as the sexual encounter itself. Remember the arcline? In the bliss and warmth of the postcoital bed, you will be tempted to roll over and sleep. Don't do it! As much as you love that feeling, that coziness with your partner, it's also the most vulnerable time for you and your arcline. Have you ever woken up the next day after what seemed to be the greatest sex—or the most intimate exchange—and felt awful? Have you wondered how this could possibly be, especially after such a delightful experience with your partner the night before? Well, that is what it feels like when you don't get up and take care of yourself and your arcline. After you've had sex, your partner will unwittingly pour his subconscious agendas, insecurities, and inner anger into you. Don't blame him; he's completely unaware of this exchange. In fact, he's probably already sleeping! But this is one of the ways that a woman's spiritual anatomy can weaken her radiance, rather than strengthen it. She must take the time to tend to it, right after sex.

What does tending to it mean? First, help your partner fall asleep. Then get up. Urinate. Wash your hands, face, back of the neck, and feet with cold water. Soak a washcloth in warm water and rinse your vagina, anus, and perineum. Then do a few stretches, set your Navel Point with Stretch Pose; lie on your back and lift your head and feet six inches. Do a few Bundle Rolls, which strengthen and seal the aura. Lie on the ground with your arms straight and stiff along the sides of your body and begin rolling left and right. Practice a pranayam for 2 or 3 minutes, and then meditate. Once you feel grounded and fully back in your body, lie down and sleep.

In this way, you nurture and support your entire energetic body and, in turn, strengthen the dynamic of your relationship.

Sex is an act of the Sixth Chakra—the Third Eye—the pituitary, the master gland of the body. This Sixth Chakra stimulates the sexual organs, then the hormones rally, and voilà—you are aroused, your senses are acute, everything is magnified. Your projection is set to merge with your partner. In this projection, your ego dies, which I believe is one reason that the orgasm is known as "the little death." This merger, this union, is the most intimate act you can share with another being; it is so profound that, without commitment, it can be extraordinarily harmful. If this "union" arises only from the Second Chakra, then you're just an animal acting on impulse. Instead of creating true union and experiencing the bliss of complete surrender, it generates enormous insecurity. That little death, which is meant to elevate and uplift into ecstasy, can instead challenge the psyche so profoundly that the energy created simply drains the two participants, rather than healing them. But if the union comes from the projection of the Third Eye—the Sixth Chakra—and unites the two souls through intention, devotion, and prayer at the Heart Center, then it is the most beautiful creation on Earth. Each sexual act has the potential to create an energy, a force, that heals. You can feel it. This true merger is one of the gifts of sexuality and intimacy. This is grace.

For couples who experience an inability to connect or create intimacy, or who've experienced a recent break in their connection, this is a wonderful exercise to bring them back to each other without the weight of roles, identity, or ego getting in the way. Instead, you merge in the breath. You unite in the gaze. You become one.

Grace Note

Let's return to the metaphor of the sea. Imagine standing on a beach; it's midnight. Allow your clothes to fall to the sand as you step out into the endless ocean. The water is warm—the same temperature as your skin. Walk deeper and deeper into the sea, away from the shore, away from any notion of who you are. Begin to lose your sense of self; allow the boundary of where your body ends and the ocean begins to slip away from you. Allow yourself to merge into the sea of the Self. Float on your back. Gaze at the stars. Empty yourself. Breathe deeply and become one with the sea and the stars.

Now take this same practice of merger into the bedroom with your partner. This doesn't involve sex; instead it is a profound surrender into the other's being through the breath and the gaze. Lie down next to each other— spooning—and begin breathing together. Inhaling and exhaling together until you lose the sense of you and the other; there is only the breath coming in and going out. Feel your partner's belly against the small of your back; feel your own belly beneath your partner's hand. Inhale and exhale; merge in the breath. Now turn and face one another. Look into each other's eyes and continue breathing together. Merge into one another's eyes. Continue to breathe consciously, together, in concert, in unison.

Opening up to your own sexuality and relishing your newfound confidence can be one of the more profound acts of freedom for any woman. Give yourself the opportunity to experience this kind of intimacy, this quality of merger, the bliss of union as an expression of your love for the divine—in yourself and your beloved. This is your grace.

Chapter Four

The Art of Living

Aging Gracefully

Some people think life is how it is, but really life is how you deal with it.[12]
—*Yogi Bhajan*

Understanding the body's rhythms is the key to good health and vitality—at every age. Yogi Bhajan described a woman's relationship to her life and her life's cycles as being in command of the flow. A woman's capacity to be in rhythm and to stay in rhythm can determine her security, her happiness, and her health. A woman's identity becomes her soul's song, the rhythm that carries her through every change and challenge.

12 © The Teachings of Yogi Bhajan, July 9, 1982

We're all familiar with the body's rhythms, despite all the attempts by our contemporary culture to tell us there's something wrong with those rhythms. What if we approached our cycles as something to master, rather than something to suppress, ignore, or dread? What would change in our relationships to ourselves and to our priorities if we respected what our cycles have to teach us? Our cycles can often be our best teachers—knowing when to rest or when to push ourselves just a little harder; listening to what our body needs and respecting it; tuning in to our particular sensitivities on any given day; listening to our emotions but understanding that some arguments are best left to another day. Our cycles teach us to experience the flow; our consciousness allows us to command that flow.

Living in Rhythm

Maintaining a rhythm that supports you and your consciousness means consciously relating to the rhythms of life: the rhythm of the day, the cycles of the moon, the changing of the seasons. Each of these rhythms affects your life in ways both large and small. Most of us have lost touch with these natural rhythms. Urban life, especially among the young, has no night or day; it's become a 24-hour world. Even life in rural communities has lost much of its connection to the land. But these natural rhythms have existed since the beginning of time. Although their importance may have gotten lost, restoring rhythm to your own life depends first upon recognizing nature's rhythms.

Each 24-hour cycle has its own internal rhythm, and each part of the day brings its own qualities and energies. These are known in ancient Indian philosophy as the *doshas*, each of which has its own particular qualities—*pitta*, which is fire; *kapha*, which contains both earth and water elements; and *vata*, which blends ether and air. These three doshas profoundly affect different parts of the day and, depending on your habits, can either disrupt or support the natural cycle. If you want to be able to sleep well, you need to be in bed before 10 p.m., before the end of the kapha cycle. If you wait much longer than that, the energy of the day begins to shift to a more active, energetic cycle—pitta—and you will find it much harder to fall asleep. If you want to have a productive day, you need to rise *before* the sun; otherwise, you will sleep through the vata cycle, which often means bad dreams and lots of tossing and turning. Even worse, you'll awaken during the kapha cycle, leaving you lethargic well into the morning hours. If you want to promote good digestion and assimilation of your food, then you should have your largest meal of the day around noon. This is the height of the sun's energy and that fire—pitta—will help support digestion and elimination, which are the keys to good health and vitality. Each day moves through these cycles; if respected, they serve to support your physical and mental vitality and well-being.

The moon cycle has a significant influence in a woman's life because of her menstruation cycle. Her connection to the full and new moons, the waxing and waning, reflects her own waxing and waning energies and moods. Her hormones are profoundly affected by the cycle of the moon. According to Yogi Bhajan, "Your biofeedback cycle moves from full moon to new moon, and then new moon to full moon. That's natural."[13]

At the full moon, your glandular system is naturally accelerated, and you experience a peak in energy; at the new moon, your energy is at its lowest; on the eleventh day of each moon, you experience balance. The ancient Ayurvedic texts describe this eleventh day (which occurs twice—once in the full moon cycle and once in the

---

13 © The Teachings of Yogi Bhajan, August 1, 1996, *Master's Touch* (Santa Cruz, NM: Kundalini Research Institute, 2000)

new moon cycle) as twilight, or a moment when the mind, which is ruled by the moon, comes to rest in one of its two homes: the Third Eye or the Heart Center.

One way to be more in tune with this cycle is to fast on lemon water from sunrise to sunset on specific days during the cycle.[14] The eleventh day of the new and full moons is a traditional day for fasting. You can also fast on the new moon and full moons themselves. Break the fast at the end of the day with a light meal of steamed greens and rice or fruit with a little plain yogurt. These short, single-day fasts support deep meditation in addition to strengthening the organs and challenging the endocrine system, restoring vitality and balance. Single-day fasts are also good for the digestive system, giving it a break from the literal "daily grind."

I find these single-day fasts particularly helpful because I have a tendency to overeat—emotional eating, anyone? Whether you crave those salty, fatty foods or you're a sweet tooth with a special place in your heart for Belgian dark chocolate, you sometimes eat to fill up something inside yourself that has nothing to do with hunger. A simple one-day fast can break the cycle of overeating and help restore balance to your relationship with food. The breath exercise that follows can also bring more balance to the moon cycle.

The cycle of the seasons also affects our rhythms. As we move through the traditional four seasons, our bodies must make adjustments to the cold, the wind, the heat, the lack of light. The shift from one season to another is often a vulnerable time for the body; it often results in an increase in allergies and colds during the spring and fall seasons. Deep systemic cleansing is recommended to help the body make these adjustments. By taxing the body as

---

14 Note: Because our systems are so sensitive, it's best to refrain from fasting longer than one day; extended fasts take a woman out of balance and are very challenging for the body to come back from.

Grace Note

If fasting isn't your thing, try this simple pranayam[1] (breath meditation) to help restore rhythm to the moon cycle. Before you begin, let's introduce the different parts of the practice.

The breath: The inhale and exhale through the nose in 8 equal beats—4 segmented breaths in (short sniffs) and 1 long exhale out (equaling 4 beats).

The mudra: With each sniff, press the tips of your fingers against the thumb, starting with the forefinger and ending with the pinkie finger.

The mantra: The words Saa Taa Naa Maa represent the cycle of life, the ongoing rhythm of birth and death. These are the seed sounds of our bij mantra Sat Nam, "Truth Is My Identity". Bij means seed and within it is contained the entire creation: Saa—infinity, Taa—life, Naa—death or transformation, Maa—birth.

Tune in, then close your eyes and sit with a straight spine. Rest your hands on your knees, palms up. Begin the segmented breath in, moving your fingers and mentally vibrating the different sounds with each sniff of the

1   From *Breath Rhythm to Regulate the Menstrual Cycle* in I AM A WOMAN: *Essential Kriyas for Women in the Aquarian Age* (Santa Cruz, NM: Kundalini Research Institute, 2009)

little as possible, through what we eat and drink, we allow the body's natural reserves to be restored and replenished before the more extreme seasons of winter and summer arrive. Depending on where you live, these particular cycles may or may not apply. But regardless of your latitude and longitude, every woman has a rhythm, just as each day has a rhythm.

breath and press of the fingertips: Saa—thumb and forefinger; Taa—thumb and middle finger; Naa—thumb and ring finger; Maa—thumb and pinkie finger. Start with 5 minutes, and increase over time, up to 31 minutes.

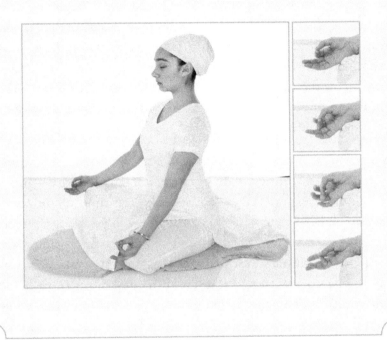

Rhythm is also about proportion. How much of your day do you work, rest, and play? Are they in balance? In today's world, where women are expected to be able to do it all, it can be challenging to find a balance. It helps to understand life's natural cycles and make conscious choices about how to express your Self within them. For example, young women are putting off marriage and family so that they can first focus on their career. Likewise, women who have the luxury of not working full time are beginning to choose flexible hours or part-time work so that they can have more time for family when their children are young. These choices, though difficult to make, are the keys to finding balance.

Women at the peak of their careers sometimes begin to define themselves by their work and lose their connection to their creativity, spontaneity, and, ultimately, their vitality. In a similar way, older women often lose their sense of purpose when they no longer have the demands of children and work. This is why it's so important for every woman to stay in touch with her creativity—at every stage of life.

Every woman is a dancer, an artist, a singer, a poet; every woman is creative. It's a critical part of every woman's identity—and it's important to express that identity. Take the time to simply be: take long hikes in nature or regular walks with your dogs; attend a pottery class at your local community college; start a blog or write in a personal journal; dust off your old camera; take a yoga class; play the piano again or for the first time; volunteer in your local community. It doesn't really matter what you do—only that you do it! Find your flow, live in rhythm. This is your grace.

Feed the Soul First

Part of establishing your rhythm is in how you start your day— consciously or not? Take the time each and every day to tune in to your soul; unite with the One, the divine within, and cultivate a relationship to the Self. Become aware of your body, challenge your ego, and align with your purpose. Our lives are so full: work, family, community service, personal pursuits, friends, and more. Give yourself this gift, first thing every morning; give yourself the time to align yourself with your Self, align your emotions with your consciousness, and align your body to its purpose, giving it the energy, vitality, and flexibility it needs to serve you throughout the day.

Start small. Give yourself a chance to succeed—a chance to feel good. The rewards of the practice will prove more than enough to keep you going: feeling more balanced throughout the day, anticipating and solving problems before they arise, enjoying increased physical energy and mental acuity. Other benefits of a daily routine include decreased pain; fewer headaches; more restful, deep sleep; clearer skin; and better eating habits. A simple formula for a healthy, happy life includes prayer or intention, breath work, yoga and/or exercise, meditation, and dwelling in the sound current. Start with 11 minutes a day and then increase it over time.

Whatever your spiritual background or beliefs, these elements can be incorporated in a way that both serves your consciousness and honors your path. For example, begin your day by offering a simple prayer—that is, dedicate your day to something higher. Then breathe long and deep, noticing the breath as it comes in and as it goes out; connect to the breath as your source of vitality and strength—your connection to life. Sustain that connection throughout your day. Now exercise: A woman must break a sweat on her brow every day to remain healthy and vital. Include some stretches and strength training as well. Kundalini Yoga as taught by Yogi Bhajan® is the perfect combination of strength, balance, and physical challenge—and yes, you will break a sweat! Then sit and meditate, still your mind, slow your breath; or find a more active meditation using movement. Either way, find a way to come to zero, or *shuniya*—for from nothing, everything arises. This is your key to prosperity. Finally chant or sing or listen to elevating music.

If you walk to work, you can chant with each step; if you drive to work, you can chant with a recording that you find uplifting and peaceful; if you take public transportation, smile at your neighbor, experience the sounds around you, and meditate on those sounds as music, as their own melody. This is grace.

Grace Note

A beautiful way to start the day is with a self-blessing. Combining prayer and meditation with awareness and self-healing, this blessing allows you to start your day from a place of deep gratitude for your life and the gifts of the body. When you wake in the morning, take a deep inhalation and cover your eyes with your hands. Then slowly open your eyes and give thanks for the ability to see. Exhale. Inhale and massage your ears, giving thanks that you can hear. Exhale. Inhale and stroke your arms, giving thanks for their strength and all they do for you each day. Exhale. Inhale and caress your hands, giving thanks for their dexterity and skill. Exhale. Inhale and touch your legs, giving thanks that they carry you out into the world each day to serve. Exhale. Inhale and massage your feet, giving thanks for all the miles they've crossed. Exhale. Inhale and continue to bless each and every part of your body. Bring awareness and healing to each organ, tissue, muscle, and bone. This is gratitude. This is grace.[1]

1 From *Self-Blessing and Awakening Exercises,* © The Teachings of Yogi Bhajan

The Rhythm of the Life Cycles

In the same way that we need to establish a rhythm in our daily lives, throughout the moon cycles, and throughout the four seasons, we also have to understand the rhythms of our life cycles. Maybe it's just me, but do you ever look back and think, Who was that? I remember what I felt like when I was 10 and think, Where'd she go? Or I think back to when I was in my 20s and wonder what could have led me on that particularly painful journey. Not that I would change anything—who I was then has brought me to where I am now. But thinking back leads me to reflect on identity and how it serves the rhythm of life.

Is the person I am now somehow fundamentally different from that 10-year-old, that 27-year-old? Is there some point in the life cycle that is essentially me, my essence, my true Self? Am I more myself as that young girl? Will I be more myself when I'm 55? These questions are interesting because throughout the various life cycles, we face particular challenges—unique to that age or cycle—that make us question our identity. The true question becomes this: In those moments when we are tested, do we have an unwavering connection to our identity, to the truth of who we are and our values? Is that connection strong enough to render opposition or coercion powerless? The rhythm of our identity is found in our song, our story, our rhythm, our expression. It is a steady beat of consciousness that doesn't waver in the face of challenges, but rather grows deeper and more profound over time.

Identity as a rhythm, as a steady current of virtue and value, as a melody that returns us again and again to our deepest truths about ourselves—that we are the Grace of God—is the key to successfully navigating the life cycles and emerging as the truest expression of our Self and our destiny. This is grace.

Grace Note

Take a moment to find your touchstone—your true identity. Stand in your center. Become still. Breathe deeply. Feel your feet connected deeply to the mother Earth. Make a connection to the Heavens through the crown of your head. Place your hands at your Navel Point. Let the breath move beneath your hands. Meditate on the words: "I am the light of my soul; I am beautiful; I am bountiful; I am bliss; I am, I am." Let these words echo and vibrate in every cell of your body; allow the melody of your identity to be the rhythm of your destiny.

Return to this meditation any time you're confronted with a choice. Stand in your center. Find your touchstone and ask yourself, "Does this serve my soul's highest destiny? Will this reflect my truest Self? Is this who I am?" Know who you are: I am, I am. I am the Grace of God. And then take action—without any reservations.

As children, most of us didn't grow up with the technologies of cold showers, massage, and bundling to strengthen our nervous system. Many of us weren't even breastfed. In fact, if you were anything like me, you grew up on Cheerios and TV! Tragically, some children don't even grow up with their own parents, or if they did, the environments weren't safe, much less ideal or cozy. We can't go back and change those things, but we can recognize the cycles we were confronted with and bring new awareness and even compassion, where needed, to reframe the past and transform the present.

Statistically eight women out of ten are damaged during their first lifecycle—that is, before they are eighteen. The rest of their life they take their vengeance. I believe in what Jesus said: "When I was a child I acted as a child, but now that I am an adult, I must act as an adult." By nature, you have to understand that if you want to live in grace, you have to let the past be past and start your life now.[15]

– Yogi Bhajan

If we don't have a secure sense of Self, if we don't have a place within us—a core Self to relate to—we can easily become confused or filled with anxiety as we pass through our various life cycles. How do we help our daughters to trust their identity, even in the face of overwhelming pressure from the outside? Recognize that your role as a parent is to usher your daughter to her destiny, not claim her as your own. Provide the environments that will flourish her creativity and curiosity, while also reinforcing her identity and security. Teach her simple ways to manage her emotions and commotions—cold showers, deep breathing, walking and chanting. Begin encouraging self-discipline while she's still young—early morning meditation, artistic expression, and community service. These core values and virtues will serve her and her identity as she grows and continues to confront the challenges, from both inside and out.

A child's first teacher is her mother. Up until the age of 3, the mother is a child's primary teacher. The environments she provides— peaceful home, cozy environments, healthy foods—make a significant impact on a child's future security and identity. After the age of 3, the father takes on a more influential role, providing a different aspect of security and identity. At the age of 7, children face their first major life cycle—the cycle of consciousness—and an entirely new reference point—peers. The primary teacher no

---

15 © The Teachings of Yogi Bhajan, July 6, 1981

longer resides at home but at school, in friends and peer groups and the pressures they exert. It's often at this point that a child also comes up against her own notion of God and where she fits in the greater picture of the world. Her sense of justice is challenged, and her understanding of what's right and what's wrong faces its first compromises. In my own life, this was a moment of profound awareness; I knew that I had lost something significant and would spend the rest of my life trying to find it.

The second major life cycle, the cycle of intelligence, begins at age 11. At this point, a child's intellect is at the beginning of its arc, which will peak at age 22. She learns quickly; the word *precocious* comes to mind. Most young girls have communication skills far beyond their age. At this age, they assimilate new information, learn to discern opposing positions, and begin to confront conventional wisdom. For my part, I loved correcting my teachers. Evidently I was an editor from a very early age! For most young girls, it's the first time they oppose their mothers, which can be painful for both the parent and the child.

The second cycle of consciousness ends at age 14, at about the same time that many girls get their first period. At this age, a young girl enters the realm of womanhood—whether she likes it or not! This new consciousness, this awareness of her capacity to create, and the longing to merge that accompanies that consciousness, awakens with the onset of new hormones. Her system is flooded with new emotions, simply because of a shift in her chemical makeup. How can her identity, her internal rhythm, make a difference against this apparent onslaught? At this point, a girl's identity probably comes up against its greatest test, and the shock of the transition leaves her vulnerable, insecure, and even lonely. But it doesn't have to be this way. By incorporating ceremony to support this emerging identity with a sense of continuity and integrity—family, home, values—we can teach her to be aware of her spiritual anatomy (see Chapter Two) and help her build on those behaviors that support her identity. If we make this a powerful transition in a girl's life, it can become an awakening—a grace.

The next major life cycle is at age 18; this completes the first cycle of life. Approaching this point, a young woman has gone through the often-crushing experience of adolescence. For girls, the years between 11 and 18 in particular are filled with insecurity and uncertainty about their bodies; the notion of beauty; the competing interests of boys versus hitting the books; myriad anxieties provoked and compounded by the constant push from peers, family, and the wider culture to look a certain way, act a certain way, be a particular kind of girl.

Once a young woman has made it through these unenviable firsts, she enters another cluster of changes in the cycles. Following that first complete life cycle at 18, she experiences her third cycle of consciousness at 21; and at 22, her second cycle of intelligence. These cycles accompany some significant shifts in a young woman's physical and mental experience of her Self and her world. Entering a new life cycle means that her physiology will begin to completely change; the things she used to be able to eat with impunity will now be a challenge to her metabolism. At this age, a young woman's sexual maturity is still developing as well (she will reach full maturity at 25); it's best if the rhythm of her identity remains within herself. That is, the longer she's willing to wait, the better her initial sexual experiences will be, and the more longevity she'll experience as a creative, sexual being as she grows older.

The years 18 to 22 are her peak years intellectually; they also provide the best opportunity to develop those positive habits that will serve her later. If a young woman can establish a rhythm at this point in her life, she will give herself the greatest chance for good health, true happiness, and success throughout her life. But for most of us, these years usually represent the exact opposite: rebellion in the form of drugs and alcohol, combined with stressful periods of late-night study sessions and equally stressful eating habits. These years often tax our system more than we imagine, and we don't experience the payback until our 30s.

Up to this point, a young woman's family and her peers have been her teachers. For a woman to reach beyond the boundaries of her attachments and her home, however, she must begin to seek a deeper relationship to the Self. The relationship to a Spiritual Teacher is part of the progressive rhythm of identity and developing consciousness in any young woman. This is a time for intensive study of the Self and the world. This is a time for her to begin singing her own true song; this is the time to begin finding her own voice; this is the time to begin joining in the chorus of the world.

Many people have heard of Saturn's Return in one context or another. For those of us who've gone through it, we often recognize (after the fact) what a tremendous shift we experienced in our late 20s and early 30s. At 28, a woman has completed the fourth cycle of consciousness; in many ways, the path she takes from that point on determines much of her adulthood experiences. For many women, marriage and family become the focus of their lives. For others, work becomes more meaningful, and they define a deeper relationship to their Self through what they do. They make a deeper commitment to their careers, or they change careers altogether and go back to school. For those of us who didn't make the greatest choices in our 20s, these years represent a huge personal transformation. Some of us get sober; some of us begin taking better care of our health;

some of us find our spiritual path, again or for the first time. Whatever you do, this new cycle of consciousness means radical shifts—whether or not you're aware of them. Find your rhythm, even in the midst of what may look and feel like chaos.

At 36, women complete their second life cycle. This is when the poor habits of youth really begin to catch up. My digestion shut down for an entire year! For many women, this time of life is a real wake-up call. Positive habits they'd been meaning to cultivate, but just never got around to, begin to call to them more urgently. A woman can see 40 from here—and depending on where they're standing, it can look pretty good or fairly scary. If you are at this stage, now is the time to begin supplementing your diet, if you haven't already, with the vitamins and oils your body needs to stay vital, balanced, and rejuvenated. High-quality, cold-pressed oils; freshly ground flaxseed; chlorophyll or other "green" food supplements; vitamin Bs; turmeric root; and a daily multivitamin are all you really need. These supplements can make a big difference in how you experience being in your body. Less pain, more energy, regular elimination, and greater resilience in your skin and connective tissues are some of the benefits of this regimen. In addition, incorporate more greens, beets, nuts, whole grains, and plain yogurt into your diet. These simple things will help sustain you, especially as your social commitments, family, and career obligations begin to weigh on you. The years from 36 to 56 can grow very, very busy, making it easy to lose sight of the important things. Slow down and tune in to your rhythm. Return to your song. This is your grace.

The next major shift in a woman's life occurs during her 50s. All three cycles converge at ages 54, 55, and 56. Much like Saturn's Return, this time can prove to be a very transformative—and challenging—time. At this stage, a woman is still young, with

Grace Note

One of the single most important meditations that Yogi Bhajan gave for women is a simple affirmation practice: I Am Grace of God.[1] Practiced throughout a woman's life, it brings light and radiance to a woman's aura, confirms her identity in the Infinite, and delivers grace to her surroundings. This practice is recommended especially for women in menopause; it helps make up for the loss of estrogen by restoring the flow and the melody to a woman's vibration.

Tune in and then lie on your back and relax. Inhale deeply, hold the breath, and mentally vibrate "I am Grace of God" ten times. Then exhale completely and hold the breath out as you mentally vibrate "I am Grace of God" ten times. Continue repeating the mantra ten times on the inhale and ten times on the exhale for a total of five inhalations and five exhalations. This totals 100 silent repetitions of the affirmation. Now sit up and bring your left hand up by your shoulder, as if you were taking an oath. Rest your right hand on your knee, palm up, with the thumb and forefinger pressed together. With your left hand:

Tense your pinkie finger as you meditate on the qualities of Mercury, the flow of water and your power to communicate. Now say aloud: I am Grace of God.

Tense your ring finger as you meditate on the qualities of the Sun, its radiance and energy expressed in your physical health, vitality, and beauty. Now say aloud: I am Grace of God.

1 From The *Grace of God Meditation* in *I AM A WOMAN: Essential Kriyas for Women in the Aquarian Age* (Santa Cruz, NM: Kundalini Research Institute, 2009)

many more productive years ahead of her; but for many, this is also a time to take a step back and decide how to spend those years. If you are at this stage, it's natural to want to begin giving back. You've fulfilled your obligations with joy, and you've reaped the

Tense your middle finger as you meditate on the qualities of Saturn, the movement of air and wind as expressed in your emotions when tempered with patience and devotion. Now say aloud: I am Grace of God.

Tense your forefinger as you meditate on the qualities of Jupiter, its etheric wisdom and expansion, and your capacity for change. Now say aloud: I am Grace of God.

Tense your thumb as you meditate on the qualities of the Earth, your groundedness and your identity. Now say aloud: I am Grace of God.

Inhale deeply and relax for a few moments, meditating in silence and in the vibration of your own True Self and your own true song.

benefits. Now you want to find a way to give your skills and your talents to something greater. For a lot of women, this is a time to find their voices once again and to lend that voice to social justice, peacemaking, or simply reaching out and mentoring young girls in the surrounding community.

Keeping your rhythm and your grace—singing your song—will be invaluable in maintaining your long-term relationships during this time. Because of the loss of hormones due to menopause, your rhythm is especially important now. Your relationship to your melody, your grace, and your identity will keep you in the flow and soften the edges that naturally arise with this new chemical profile. Remember the torrent of emotions and commotions upon the onset of these same hormones? Well, learning to live without them again is equally challenging. Call upon your song and dwell in the rhythm of your identity: I am Grace of God.

This identity—the Grace of God—will carry you through the remainder of your life, as you become the wise woman, serving the community, serving your family, and exploring in these last best years your creativity, self-expression, and joy. My grandmother completed countless quilts and even took up painting in her final years. My own mother began painting again in her late 60s and early 70s, among her many other creative pursuits. Others travel and serve people around the world with skills they've cultivated their entire lives: healing, teaching, engineering, providing legal aid, and more. Of this stage in life it can be said that the wise woman knits the world together with her acts of kindness. She holds the world up through her prayer. She sings the world a song of peace and prosperity, dignity, and divinity. She sings to the world "Awake!" even as she prepares her own soul for sleep.

Find your rhythm, your flow, your song—this is your identity, which remains true from the beginning to the end. Walking in rhythm, living in harmony, dwelling in prosperity—these are the keys to happiness. This is your grace.

Chapter Five

The Art of Communication

The Word and the Sword

Remember: the Word is God and God is the Word. You are what your words are.[16]

—*Yogi Bhajan*

A woman's word is very powerful. It is, in fact, her most powerful creative force, as well as her most destructive weapon. A woman's word has impact. Yet somehow, we've lost the art of communication. Most modern women have lost touch with how powerful their word can be—how potentially transformative their communications are.

16 © The Teachings of Yogi Bhajan, August 25, 1978

We've been so focused on gender equality that we've lost touch with the power of graceful, polite communication; we've lost the art of communicating *as a woman*. Men never forget that they came from a woman, that they were nursed by a woman, taught by a woman, and guided by a woman. Therefore, in communication with a man, we have an advantage. Thus one of the first principles in the art of communication is not to abuse that advantage, not to misuse or misdirect our power through manipulation or control. Instead we need to trust and communicate directly, with kindness, clarity, and compassion.

I can hear the clamor of feminists everywhere—and I consider myself one, mind you. But as my father often said to me, "You catch more flies with honey than with vinegar." I, of course, balked at the Southern sensibility that this saying invoked, and in my cynical way, I thought to myself, "Who wants flies?" But now, years later, as a woman who has had both successful and unsuccessful communications at work, in relationships, and in the world as a teacher and performer, I see the truth of his words. Diplomacy is an underrated skill; but as women, we're naturals! We've simply lost touch with our sensitivity and intuition. We've lost touch with our grace.

A key component to experiencing our grace, rhythm, and identity is through sound—finding our voice, singing our song. It is the thread that runs through every part of a woman's life. It is our graciousness, our kindness, our sweetness; it is a sound like music. It is the nectar of life. It is the Grace of God. Sound is the purest and simplest way to heal and transform. As a science, sound uses the body as a vibratory chamber to come into union with the One—the ecstatic experience and steady grace that mark awakening. As women grow older, sound is a way to sustain that nectar, that sweetness. As young women, that nectar is the key to radiance and beauty. And in young girls, that nectar is their joy, creativity, and security.

Merging with and mastering the flow of the sound current are the keys to a woman maintaining and communicating her grace—at every age and stage of life. What does mastering the sound current mean? Well, within the context of Kundalini Yoga, it means mastering mantra, experiencing *simran* (meditation), and merging with the *anahat* (unstruck sound). These are fairly sophisticated concepts, though. How can we incorporate these subtle gifts into our daily lives, our daily exchanges, and our communications?

The simplest way to think about the sound current in your everyday life is through your voice—the quality, tone, and timbre of your voice says so much about you. Do you struggle to be heard? Do you use your voice to flirt? Does your voice still sound like a child's, rather than a woman's? Does your voice have an edge to it? These qualities, among others, point to specific constructs within your projection: shyness, hidden agendas, unwillingness to grow up, or unresolved anger. Coming into a conscious relationship with your voice can be a tool to transforming the way you communicate to the world. Learning to speak from the Navel Point, opening your heart and throat to your true sound, your true voice, will connect you to a deeper sense of your Self and a truer sense of your identity. Your rhythm will be steadier, your melody will be sweeter, and your communications will be clearer—because you will be you!

This next exercise will help clear and open the Fifth Chakra and connect you to your Navel Point at the Third Chakra. The combination of these two energies makes for effective speech and strength in your projection.

Grace Note

Explore your voice. Begin by just saying your name aloud. Hear your name as you speak it. Become aware of your body, your breath, and your surroundings. This is your checkpoint.

Take a moment to explore your own sound. Inhale deeply; then simply open your mouth and sing, "Aaaaahhhhhhh." Be sure to open your jaw wide. Relax your face. Tune in to your Heart Center. Feel the sound in your body. Notice your emotions. Now take that simple sound, "ah," and move it up and down the scale, or sing a simple melody. Engage the Navel Point and sing. Now move the sound down and sing from your tailbone. Move the sound up and sing from your Third Eye. Just experience the sound—the full range of your voice.

Take a deep breath and hold in your mind's eye the truest thing you know about yourself. On the exhale, say your name. Listen to the sound from this true place. Engage your Navel Point and say your name again. Become aware of your body, your breath, and your surroundings. Notice the difference from the beginning of the exercise to now—this is your voice; this is your grace.

Return to this exercise again and again as you explore the depth of your sound and the strength of your identity as it's reflected and projected through your voice.

As women, we must accept the potency of our words. Our words can heal or destroy. Every day, in our relationships, at work, and within ourselves, we make that choice. Consciously or unconsciously, our words serve to heal or to destroy. If we are conscious of it, we can cut through the karma and have the opportunity to live fully in our purpose. When unconscious—or worse, driven by subconscious agendas—we generate unintended consequences. We generate more karma. I often talk about things coming out sideways— that is, if I'm uncomfortable or if something has triggered me and I'm out of balance, that agitation and discomfort will come out sideways. I'll take it out on someone or something that has nothing to do with what triggered me or with what I'm experiencing within myself. The test is to apply the balm of our words or the sword of our tongue to our lives with consciousness. There are times and opportunities when a woman's word—her sword—can be her most powerful tool: to be blunt, to cut through the proverbial bullshit, to create a clear boundary. This is a woman's strength; this is a woman's grace. But there are other times when her word can act as a soothing balm. As a woman, you must have mastery over when you apply the salve versus when you apply the sword.

Yogi Bhajan often said, "In the beginning was the word."[17] In this way, he was recognizing the creative power and projection inherent in language. It is through the word that we create our world. It is through the word that we create love, prosperity, and peace. It is through the word that we promulgate hate, greed, and corruption. It is through the word that we seek reconciliation and

17 John 1:1

forgiveness. It is through the word that we generative divisiveness and separation. Everything manifests through the word. Our world and our perceptions are colored by our language. Change the way we speak about ourselves and others, and we can change the world.

Let's begin by observing how we speak to and about ourselves as women. One of the first principles of prosperity is never to speak negatively about yourself—or anyone else. How many of us can say we live this law of prosperity? Certainly not me. But because of our negativity, we are limiting ourselves, the flow of the Universe, and, in turn, our opportunities. In many ways, we are culturally conditioned to think, speak, and act negatively toward ourselves. Nothing is good enough; we are a culture of the perfect, the ideal—a fanaticism imposed upon the feminine form by commerce and the male subconscious agenda. Women participate in this systemic misogyny here and around the world. But we have to turn it around. We have to communicate self-love—toward our own bodies, toward our own nature, toward the divine within us.

Speaking & Listening Exercises

Yogi Bhajan gave two simple exercises to bring awareness to how we talk to ourselves: mirror exercises and recording yourself. In the first exercise, you sit before a mirror and simply have a conversation with your Self. Be as honest and open as you can. Listen to the thoughts that arise and observe. Is this your voice? Your mother's? Your father's? Is it affirming and uplifting? Is it cutting and negative? Just notice. Practice 11 minutes a day, simply looking into a mirror and having a heart-to-heart talk with your Self. As the practice continues, allow the negative self-talk to fall away and begin to reach a place of true intimacy and authenticity within your Self and your Soul. After this practice, it's much easier to apply this same awareness to how you talk about yourself to others, as well as how you create positive boundaries for yourself and how you let people talk to you.

In the second exercise, simply record yourself for one full day. Everything you say—all day. Then sit and listen and make notes about how often you put yourself down, how often you compliment yourself, how you interact with others, and how they respond to you. Look at the ratio of negative and positive communications, self-negating versus self-promoting speech— and observe your reactions to each. For many people, this exercise comes as a shock. Most of us have very little idea how negative we are about ourselves. We're often our own worst critic. Listening to and observing how you speak about yourself can be one of the most transformative experiences you'll ever have, especially in regard to how you communicate with yourself and others.

"A woman who does not speak through her radiance is not a woman."[18] When a woman resides in her radiance, it's impossible for her to speak or act from her negativity. In turn, when a woman is negative and speaking from her attachment or need for control, in that moment she is not a woman; that is, she isn't in her highest consciousness. This doesn't mean that a woman can't confront or cut; it means that when she is in her radiance, any negativity is delivered consciously, with the intention to challenge, transform, and elevate.

18 © The Teachings of Yogi Bhajan, circa 1978

Grace Note

Practice this pranayam before going to bed in order to relax more deeply and sleep more soundly, which helps rebuild the nerves and, in turn, increase your radiance. Tune In. Sit in a comfortable posture with a straight spine; hands in your lap, palms up, with your right hand resting in your left. Your thumbs are together and point away from you. Focus your eyes on the tip of the nose, with your eyelids half-closed. Inhale in four equal parts, mentally vibrating the mantra Saa Taa Naa Maa.[1] *Hold the breath and vibrate the mantra four times (for a total of 16 beats). Exhale in two equal strokes, projecting mentally* Wahe Guru. *Pronounced* Whaa-hay Guroo, *which means "great is the ecstasy of being brought from darkness to light." Continue for 15 minutes. You can increase this practice up to 62 minutes a day if you like.*

This rhythmic mantra will eventually progress so that even in daily activities, you will automatically hear the mantra and take on the rhythm of this breath. This pranayam gives radiance, and that radiance gives patience, which is the first condition of real love. In love, you give—without attention to all the mistakes of the other—just as the sun gives light and warmth to all. The disciplined practice of this breath, known as Shabd Kriya, *incorporates this universality within the personality.*

1 See Grace Note on Page 52 for more information about the mantra from *Shabd Kriya,* © The Teachings of Yogi Bhajan, 1974.

Conscious Communication

As women, our very presence is our communication. There's so much backlash about the double-standard, and yet the polarity of male and female has been around for more than one generation. So we can't expect all those values and norms to be dropped within one generation. How you dress, how you walk, the tone of your

voice, your manner—it all communicates. And because you're always communicating, the question becomes, what do you want to communicate? Conscious communication means having a shared or "common notion." When you aren't conscious about how you present yourself, the common notion is still there; it's just subconscious. So ask yourself: "What am I communicating by the way I dress? What am I communicating in my tone? What am I saying by the way I walk? What do my mannerisms and gestures say?"

Are you willing to be conscious in how you present yourself? If you aren't, then your words have already lost 80 percent of their power and projection because so much of what you communicate is through body language. If you are willing, then your grace will carry the day, and your communications will always bring you victory. Now, here's the bitter pill: When you want to communicate with a man and you are dressed in something that even mildly shows off your body or your décolletage, the man only sees your body or imagines your breasts. He won't hear a thing—and it's not because he's a pig or a jerk, although he may be! It's his nature; just as it is in your nature to subconsciously use your body to communicate and get your way. Neither is wrong or bad—it's just our nature.

Understanding your nature is the first step to being able to get what you actually want: respect, dialogue, and conscious communication. You don't mean to communicate that you're available for sex, and yet your clothes undermine you. You don't want to communicate that you're a doormat, but your posture undermines your projection. You don't want to communicate that you're impatient or overbearing, but your tone and your gestures are dead giveaways. Becoming accountable for your communication, from head to toe, aligning your word and your actions delivers so much power to your word, your projection, and, ultimately, your ability to manifest the things you want.

A woman's innocence communicates as much as her radiance. What do I mean by innocence? Certainly not the childlike quality cultivated by a culture that wants to keep women dependent. Innocence isn't an absence of intellect or wisdom; instead, it is an attitude that trusts the flow, lives in rhythm, and elevates every circumstance. The culturally embedded, negative images of woman portray her as the "bitch;" the cynical, nagging, controlling "hag." She's parodied in the media, and men use this image to alienate themselves from their partners and their commitments. But when a woman speaks from innocence, she cuts through all these stereotypes and diffuses any negativity with the purity and clarity of her words, her tone, and her attitude. A woman's innocence always assumes the best, always elevates the dialogue, and always trusts the Infinite.

Innocence uses the diagonal to cut through the blocks—the assumptions and the cynicism—to find solutions, to communicate directly and clearly, and to deliver outcomes that benefit everyone. As a woman, you have 9 seconds to create an impact with your word. If you approach with innocence, then you've already established an advantage. You've won people over simply by your attitude. When you use graceful, soft-spoken speech, you put people at ease. You win through your innocence.

There are times, though, when your speech must be direct—and here your bluntness is indispensable. In an intimate relationship, you cannot brook evasion. If and when your gut says something's wrong, it probably is. These are the moments when, before you say anything, you must know where you stand. If you want to preserve the relationship, you must confront the evasion; but you must also elevate your partner—challenge him to rise to his caliber; challenge him to live in his integrity. Otherwise, challenge that isn't accompanied by overtures of reconciliation will only undermine the trust you've built. If you don't confront with the intention to preserve, then you only participate in the evasion. Don't undermine your own integrity; connect to the Infinite, confront the situation fearlessly, and trust that what happens is for the good.

What happens when your gift, your bluntness, is out of balance? Well, the result looks a lot like me: a strong, independent, self-confident woman who has never learned to soften her approach. Whether out of stubbornness or an unwillingness to compromise or simply the inability to change my patterns, I've never been able to adopt the soft-spoken, compassionate communication. It's an imbalance. All of us as women have both of these aspects—the blunt and the soft. And not surprisingly, I'm really a softhearted person. My bravado is simply a defense—a really old protective mechanism that doesn't seem to shift, even with all my study and meditation.

Grace Note

Tune in to your arcline. Take a deep breath and imagine the word "bitch." Feel the effect in your arcline. Exhale. Take a deep breath and imagine the word "queen." Feel the effect in your arcline. Exhale. Continue this exercise with your own examples. Experience the effect that these words have in your arcline. Now tune in and then practice this meditation:[1]

With your eyes focused on the tip of your nose, fold your hands into fists and extend the forefinger and middle finger of each hand, with your thumb holding down the ring finger and pinkie. With your elbows tucked at your sides, begin swinging your hands out and then to the center. Your fingertips will touch in front of the Heart Center. Each time your fingertips come together, chant Har, which means the creative aspect of the Divine. Continue in a steady, unbroken rhythm, swinging your hands out to your sides and then bringing the fingertips together. Practice for 3 to 11 minutes. To close, extend your right arm straight up into the sky, as though you were plugging

1 From the Meditation for the Arcline: Realize Your Power, © The Teachings of Yogi Bhajan, 1996

But at least at this point in my life, I understand the benefits of diplomatic communication. In the past, I held only scorn for what I perceived as women who were using their femininity to manipulate or cajole situations to their advantage. What I would give now for the capacity to master my projection so that I could have the advantage a soft-spoken woman has; I keep working on it! The lesson for all of us is this: Understand the advantages of your style—blunt or soft-spoken—and position your communications so that you can get the outcome that's best for everyone.

your fingers into the Universe. Bring your left arm in front of the Heart Center (parallel to the ground). Keep the mudra in your hands, and with your mind's eye, continue the movement. Concentrate. Now inhale, exhale, and relax.

Another great tool is silence. If, as a woman, you are disrespected in any way—by your partner, your colleague, your children, or anyone—the most graceful communication is silence. Simply don't acknowledge the communication or the dynamic. Disrespectful communication is so harmful to you as a woman. It penetrates your arcline and compromises your radiance. It triggers shame, anger, and other subconscious agendas within your psyche. The bottom line: It's harmful. As a woman, you shouldn't indulge it or respond to it in any way. It's unacceptable. Your silence will serve notice: "I am a graceful woman." You'll quickly find that people begin to modify their communications and begin to treat you with a newfound respect.

Conversely, however, we women cannot take the silent treatment ourselves. We can dish it, but we can't take it. This is counterintuitive, I know; but it's simply a fact. The silent treatment is the most painful thing you can do to a woman. After 72 hours, she'll do anything to break the silence. So, be judicious about using silence yourself; because if it comes back your way, you won't like it!

The meditation on page 78 strengthens the arcline at the Heart Center and allows you to experience your own power, making you less vulnerable to negative communication and charged interactions. After you've completed the practice, return to the initial visualization. Meditate on the various words and notice the effect on your arcline. Do you feel a difference? Do the words have less impact? Do you find your arcline more resilient after the meditation? Continue to practice this meditation regularly, especially if you find that your communication style is reactive or defensive in any way.

Simple meditations like this can make interactions out in the world so much easier for us to navigate. As women, it can sometimes feel like our entire culture is determined to undermine, degrade, or sexualize us by any and every means. Advertisements, sit-coms, magazine articles—you name it, the feminine form is under attack regularly, and this affects us. Don't underestimate its effect; but don't give it more power than it already has either. Create a strong, radiant body by generating a powerful arcline, and you will give yourself an opportunity to communicate with victory!

Listening—The Key to the Heart

"Purest are those who have the art of listening; those who speak the truth are pure, but those who listen to the truth are the purest."[19]

As women, we've lost the art of listening. After years of being inundated with sexual innuendo and exploitation, the only thing we hear now is desire and agenda. We are no longer able to hear a man's voice and trust him. This is the dilemma of the modern woman. For, in truth, listening is a woman's gift; it is the purest act of love; and it is what men most long for—pillow talk; someone they can trust to simply hear them out at the end of the day. Isn't that what we all want?

The art of listening delivers us to our destiny and our prosperity. The art of listening opens up the entire world: listening, we drop our pain; listening, we gain wisdom; listening, we bear the fruits of meditation; listening, we dwell in bliss.[20] Listening, true listening, requires trust; trust in our own intuition, our inner guidance, our inner voice. True listening demands a neutral mind and an open heart. True listening requires that we dwell in our purity. If we

19 © The Teachings of Yogi Bhajan, July 6, 1983
20 See the *Sunni-ai Pauris* of Japji by the 15th-century saint Guru Nanak Dev Ji

listen from that place of pain, if we listen from our past abuse and exploitation, if we listen from our hidden agendas, we're not really listening at all; we're projecting. We're listening for the Second Chakra agenda; we're listening for the negativity; we're listening for the contempt; we're listening for the hubris, the condescension; you name it, we're listening for anything but the authentic relay, which is the purpose of any communication.

True listening can heal us of our own pain and hidden agendas—and help to heal others, too. Listening begins with silence—not a punishing silence, but instead, a quality of silence that is spacious, generous, and full of equanimity. This silence allows for true, dynamic relay—otherwise known as dialogue. When you hold this kind of silence when listening, it means you're not preparing what you're going to say next. You're not assuming anything. Instead, you're simply listening.

Listening requires patience. In fact, true listening builds patience. There are so many times when someone I'm close to is going on and on and on, and I've tuned him out. Sometimes I don't even know I've tuned him out until I realize I haven't heard a word he has said! This inability to listen implies a kind of impatience and intolerance that I don't really like about myself. So, I have to ask that person to repeat what he said, and I turn my attention to listening. It's a concerted effort on my part at times, and it definitely takes practice. But the more neutral I am, the more relaxed I am; and the less attached I am to my own agenda, the better I listen.

Listening is a conscious act of service to another being. Listening builds trust. Whether it's your pet, your child, your neighbor, or your beloved, when you listen to them, they feel loved, appreciated, understood. They feel seen. And in a world in which so much information, so much noise, so much to do all make it easy to feel invisible, being seen is a gift. It is your grace.

The art of communication implies a facile quality, a deft touch, a gentle maneuvering; it is mastery. Knowing when to use your sword and when to apply a soothing salve; knowing when to listen versus when to speak; knowing when to confront and when to let go; knowing when to be silent versus when to challenge—these are the gifts of mastery. The art of communication allows you to wield your sword with grace and use your words with wisdom. This is your unique gift, and it is your grace.

Chapter Six

The Art of Relationships

Living in Harmony

Love is like the humble flow of a brook. The water keeps going at the same speed again and again, constant. It is so beautiful, so flowing, so clear, so cool, so fantastic, that in the inner heart, love springs up.[21]

—*Yogi Bhajan*

Harmony. The music of the spheres. The Golden Ratio. These ideals have been talked about by philosophers, mathematicians, and classical musicians and artists for centuries. The notion that

21 © The Teachings of Yogi Bhajan, *The Oriental Woman* (Santa Cruz, NM: Kundalini Research Institute, 1981)

Grace Note

Close your eyes. Breathe deeply. Feel the surface of your skin. Notice the temperature of the air. Notice any tension in your body. Breathe deeply again. Expand your awareness. Sense the field. Listen deeply. Now, add a thought, a word. Notice the effect on the field. Notice any shift in the vibration. Notice any change in your body. Breathe deeply again. Relax the thought. Keep repeating this simple process and notice the shifts in your body, in your breath, and in the field. Begin to sense the effect your thoughts have on yourself and on the world. Call the Heavens to Earth with every breath, and generate peace, ease, and harmony in every relationship, every particular intimacy, every interaction.

we can bring the Heavens to Earth has long been sought but never actually realized. What would it look like to call the Heavens down and begin to live in harmony here on Earth? To live in concert with another; to listen, respond, improvise—to make music. "You can live at each other, with each other, or for each other."[22] The highest manifestation of relationship is to live for each other. Each of us, whether in an intimate relationship, with our friends and family, or practicing selfless service in our communities, is called to live to this highest vibration of relationship—living *for* each other.

Every time you reach out and give your neighbor a hand, or let the car in front of you merge instead of cutting it off, or smile at the clerk behind the counter, you're making music. You are contributing harmony to the vibratory field. Each time you shout in frustration, or tail someone because you're in a hurry, or fail to look into the eyes of your waiter, you are generating discord in the vibratory

22 © The Teachings of Yogi Bhajan, a quote found often throughout his lectures on relationships and community.

field. Everything we do matters. Every thought, every action, and every failure to act has a consequence in the vibratory field. We can't predict the outcome, but we can bring consciousness, "positive vibrations," and good intention to our every action. Become a part of the field. Tune in and make music with each and everything you do. This is intercourse; this is harmony; this is grace.

Befriending the Soul

In our seemingly endless search for "our one true love," we often overlook our fundamental, core relationship—with our Self and our soul. The relationship that we establish with our own soul is the

Grace Note

Take your soul for a walk today. You don't need a destination. There's nowhere to go. Simply put on your walking shoes and head out the front door. Have a conversation. Ask your soul what it needs, what it would like to do next. Let your soul know how grateful you are that it came at this particular time and in this particular place. With each step, be grateful for what is; then, in consciousness, step into the future. Let your soul guide you. Which way should you turn? Listen to your soul. When is it time to go home? Listen to your soul. When you're most afraid, listen to your soul. Build a relationship to your Self and your soul and watch all your relationships unfold and prosper.

key to successful friendships, renewed ties to family, and ultimately, an intimate, loving long-term relationship. In fact, we'll never be able to enter a true partnership until we have taken care of our own needs first. If you enter a relationship, whether with a friend or a lover, hoping to have your own needs met, then the relationship is just a transaction; it's business. Once the need is fulfilled, the reasons for the relationship fall away and typically, it will end—and it's usually not very pretty. So the first step toward any balanced, harmonious relationship is a deep and profound connection to your Self and your soul.

Imagine spending as much time searching for your Self, cultivating your Self, and communicating with your Self as you do trying to find someone out there. Take a quick inventory: How much energy, time, and resources have you invested in trying to meet that special woman or that special man? In trying to keep them? Now, imagine spending that much time on yourself. Imagine cultivating the conversation with your own identity, exploring all the many facets that make up you, and lovingly and courageously accepting your Self—being with your Self. Because until that hole, that hunger, within you is filled with the knowledge and presence of Infinity, the You within you, the light of the soul—honestly, you don't stand a chance.

We enter relationships incomplete, looking for something to fill our own needs rather than looking for someone to love, serve, and give joy to. When we do this, what do we find? Someone who fits that particular piece of the puzzle—that particular gap within ourselves—and we call it destiny. But the destiny we need to seek is already right here inside us. The companionship, the kindness, the tenderness, the joy are all right here within us, waiting patiently for us to call upon it. This is grace.

More than 50 years ago, Anne Landers began a small column in her local newspaper, answering women's questions about relationships, marriage, and childrearing. Combine that with the consciousness movement of the 1960s and 1970s, and we see the beginnings of what is now a booming new business: advice columns about everything under the sun; armchair television therapists talking about everything from finances to relationships to sex to fitness; and an entirely new genre in publishing—self-help. The culture of "becoming your best" was born, and it hasn't been all bad. In fact, lots of good has come from it. We talk more openly about sex, we can acknowledge addiction and abuse within ourselves and our families, and we have grown more versed in the basics of human behavior so that we can begin to understand why we do what we do—and maybe even find a way to change. But it can also be exhausting! An unseen side effect has been the erosion, little by little, of friendship, of true sisterhood and brotherhood.

Friendship is one of the most beautiful ways in which human beings—and women especially—relate to each other. In today's society, friends become a self-selected family, a tribe. We depend on each other, support each other, and lift each other up, especially during the challenging times. Most of us can call someone a friend; yet, how has this barrage of advice and earnestness, this obsessive need for "improvement" changed friendships? Well, instead of just listening and supporting and being there for each other, there is often the temptation to give advice and counsel—or worse, to coerce or issue ultimatums when our "friend" isn't acting the way we think she should. Instead, *true* friendship is a willingness to share the most intimate parts of ourselves, especially those things we can't or won't share with our families or our partners. True friendship is vulnerability and acceptance. True friendship can also mean confrontation, on occasion; but in truth, a friend simply stands beside you, doesn't try to "solve" you, and cheers for you when you succeed and when you don't. Cherish your friends; cultivate the connections that serve your consciousness. This is grace.

The Sun & Moon Teachings

Man is not a woman, and woman is not a man. There is nothing common. One is moon; one is sun. One reflects; the other projects. . . It's not the same. —*Yogi Bhajan*

The nature of a woman's emotions, physiology, and life cycle has already been discussed at length. But what can we learn about ourselves in contrast to men? My favorite quote from Yogi Bhajan says, "If you don't have a man in your life to reflect, then shine like the full moon you are." So for all of us single women, we get to simply shine! But once we're in relationship—whether it's an intimate relationship or a work relationship or a relationship with a family member—if that relationship is with our polarity, a man, then we, as the feminine principle, must reflect, contain, and sustain the male polarity to create a successful, harmonious interaction or long-term relationship. We, as women, regulate the frequency of all the relationships in our lives. It's a tremendous responsibility, but it's also a gift. It is our nature; it is our grace.

What does it mean to be the moon to a man's sun? The sun shines all the time; it's constant, unwavering, and steady. This is a contributing factor to man's single-pointed nature. Men can only do one thing at a time; whereas a woman's sensory system is built for multitasking. She's built to cultivate and nurture relationships. Her arcline supports her in creating connections and containing and sustaining multiple relationships.

The moon reflects the sun's light; it waxes and wanes in relationship to the sun. What does it mean to reflect your partner? Reflecting a man means that you are attuned to his feelings, his challenges, and his physical well-being. By mirroring your partner in simple ways, matching his energy, and providing for his needs, which sometimes can be as simple as providing a glass of water, you can help him shift to a more receptive and engaged communication. Accepting his nature as the sun can also provide a lot of relief to your psyche. You can quit questioning his feelings. You can stop worrying. He's shining all the time, even if a cloud has passed over for a while. This fundamental nature of the man is also the source of his confusion when you question his feelings or devotion. He's the same; your questions only make him wonder why *you* have changed. He begins to question your loyalty, which is his number one value. In this way, women often create a vicious loop of suspicion, doubt, and insecurity in their relationships. Instead, just bask in the sun's warmth and use your sensory system to always be one step ahead of your man—and in this way, create a cozy, happy home.

What does it mean to contain and sustain a man in relationship? To contain means holding, supporting, and sustaining through your prayer, through your meditation. Remember the Adi Shakti? Remember its vastness? To contain your man means sustaining your beloved in Infinity, surrounding your beloved and your family in this vastness, and supporting your world through your prayer. It doesn't mean putting him or yourself in a box. It doesn't mean control. Reflect, contain, and sustain—this is your capacity and your caliber as a woman; this is your grace.

It's also important to understand that men and women have completely different needs in an intimate relationship. Men want admiration, trust, and, as mentioned already, loyalty. Women want security and appreciation. These are primal, core needs, meaning they don't always inspire the highest consciousness or the most rational behavior. However, if you can approach each other's needs in consciousness and, as a woman, meet your own needs through your relationship to your Self and the Divine, then you'll give yourself and your relationship the best opportunity for happiness.

Moon & Moon—Sun & Sun

For those in same-sex relationships, these same principles apply, but in a much more flexible, dynamic expression. Many same-sex relationships are played out in fairly traditional gender roles—that is, the polarity of sun and moon still exists, just more subtly. An equal number of same-sex relationships, however, depend on these traditional gender roles very little, if at all. Their connection and service to one another are expressed freely, throughout the entire range of intimacy and domestic responsibilities that make up long-term committed relationships.

Because of the freedom and flexibility afforded by same-sex relationships, gay couples often describe their relationships as being more about discovering and expressing themselves than fulfilling some preconceived notion or expectation that often comes with the title "wife" or "husband." As same-sex marriage becomes more universally accepted, it will be interesting to observe the shift, if any, in long-term gay and lesbian partnerships, once they take on the same labels and legal and social constraints as straight couples. In turn, it will be interesting to observe shifts in heterosexual marriages: will traditional gender roles change and transform as individual expression and equanimity make their way into the culture and the conversation that is marriage?

Intimacy—The Long View

If a man ever comes, let him come on your terms. Be there, by yourself, until you find a man who can fit in with you, rather than you fit in with a man.[23] —*Yogi Bhajan*

The fundamental mistake we make as modern women, which is compounded by our training when we're young, is the belief that

23 © The Teachings of Yogi Bhajan, July 9, 1979

the same behaviors we call on to establish a relationship can be used to maintain a relationship. It's simply not possible. Sustaining a long-term relationship requires a completely different set of skills, expectations, and behaviors. Of course, you may feel like you don't know how to do this! But don't worry—there's hope. If you can change how you approach the beginning of a relationship, you have a chance to not only establish a connection but also maintain and grow it over time. But this requires a real shift in how you think about and perceive relationships with men.

Dating, or checking each other out, is a set up for failure and rejection. Yogi Bhajan would often say, "In every date, there is a pit!" And typically that pit is disappointment: He doesn't call, even though he said he would, among the many others. Our contemporary culture asks us to flirt and beguile to attract the attentions of a man. This sets up a dynamic that we call romance, but that is actually just a fantasy. This dynamic communicates, "I'm for sale," which of course, you don't intend; but that's what is responded to from a deep, subconscious level in the male psyche. How can we break out of this habit of flirt and fantasy and its accompanying pain and misery? Here are six principles that will help you define a new approach to beginning relationships and provide the keys to sustaining them over time:

Test   *Contain*

Temper   *Mold*

Trust   *Preserve*

What do these six words mean in the context of establishing a meaningful relationship? Let's go through each one and see how they apply.

 ## *Test*

Instead of dating someone and falling into the trap of making yourself available, emotionally and physically, from the moment you catch each other's eye, test the man and test yourself. How does he treat you when he realizes he can't get anything from you? How does he treat the waiter or the doorman? How does he drive? My dad always had me look at their shoes (although I wouldn't want that same metric used against me!). These examples may seem mundane, but you can learn a lot about someone just by observing their small, everyday behaviors and habits.

In this introductory stage, don't believe everything you hear. Most of the time, men lie not because they are fundamentally dishonest, but because they want to please you. They want to "say the right thing." Take your time and discern the truth for yourself. Test him! See if he does what he says he will do. See if he has the caliber and the capacity to follow through. Introduce him to your friends—and believe what your friends say about him! This is so important. We so often dismiss what other people say in the mistaken belief that it won't be that way for us. This is a recipe for misery. If you can, ask those who've "dated" him before; find out what their experience was. Listen; observe.

Take this time to test yourself, too. Look for familiar signs: Are your old habits and patterns being triggered? If yes, then pause and ask yourself a question: "Is this the same guy I've always dated?" We often believe that this time will be different, which is also known as the definition of insanity—doing the same thing over and over again and expecting different results. But if you feel you've tested him and you believe he's passed, and if you're relaxed and you can be yourself with him and his family and friends, then it's time to have a conversation about commitment.

As women, we do not have the emotional, physical, or energetic capacity to bring someone into our life (our aura and arcline) without commitment *first*. Just accept it. Although it goes against everything our culture sets us up for from childhood on—love, romance, picket fences, and "happily ever after"—our experience tells us it's true. We so want to believe in "love" that we compromise our Self and discount time and time again our own nature. Without commitment, however, relationships are simply an invitation to insecurity. So have the conversation about commitment; that alone won't mean that everything will work out and you'll be singing "wine and roses." But it will mean that you haven't set yourself up to be exploited. You'll be clear about who you are and what you want, and you'll give him the opportunity to either step up and match your caliber or walk away. This testing, of yourself and the other, will save you so much heartache and pain in the long run. Trust me, I know.

 ## Temper

Once you've decided to enter into a committed relationship, then prepare to be tempered. Just like steel, you will each go through the fire. It's your job as the woman to remember the sweetness. Every fiber in your body will try to test the newfound commitment. And he'll be testing you, too—as much or more! This is when the four horsemen of the apocalypse come storming in—sabotage, insecurity, doubt, and fear—wanting to undercut your word and your commitment. During this phase, you may find yourself doing some really strange things; neurotic behaviors you thought long dormant flower again like dandelions gone to seed—they're everywhere! Don't despair. Stay open and practice compassion for yourself and your partner.

So many of us have abandonment issues in our history; we were rejected once, so we test everyone we meet to see if they're going to reject us, too. Recognize this tendency in yourself and simply stop. Don't react. Your fantasies will kick into overdrive right about now; but real relationships have nothing to do with the fantasies you grew up with, nor do they have anything to do with the "him" you've created in your mind. Relationships are about loving one another, not about getting what you want. Recognize the fantasy and drop it. Use your diagonal energy to cut through the block and reaffirm your commitment. If you can each allow yourself to be tempered, without letting go of each other's hand, you will move through this phase with grace and grit and a renewed joy and love for each other, as well as an even deeper commitment to one another.

 Trust

At this point, you'll probably find yourself in unfamiliar territory—a land called trust. Most of us never arrive here, so enjoy it! But also take care of it. As a woman, it is in your nature to want to question everything—don't. A woman gets nine questions within any 24-hour period before her partner just tunes her out. So be judicious. Practice *shuniya*—inner stillness; practice silence. Place your trust in God and then trust your partner—just trust. When you want to ask who called, breathe. I know; it's hard. For many of us, betrayal is the norm; we expect it, and in expecting it, we create it. So just as you had to go through the fires of your own neuroses and insecurities and temper yourself, you now have to wait it out and trust. Practice. Practice. Practice.

This isn't to say that you shouldn't trust your intuition; confrontation and direct, clear communication are often the only ways to address a man's wavering behaviors. But in the end, you can only be responsible for your own experiences, your own actions, and your own behaviors. And remember: The reality of a conscious relationship is that you can never be betrayed; you can only betray yourself. Believe in yourself, believe in your partner, and continue to uplift him, encourage him, and hold steady in your trust of the Infinite. Miracles will begin to happen as each new day passes and you grow in love, in trust, and in acceptance of each other—good and all.

 Contain

From the very beginnings of the relationship, you, your consciousness, and your prayer began the work of containing your man. It's a vast yet subtle task that you as a woman are uniquely suited to. It will serve you best during the tough times—and they will come. No relationship is immune from struggle. "Contain, never blame" should be your mantra throughout. It's also important to remember to congratulate yourself, especially when it's hard, because it means you've both reached a deeply committed place. You can speak for your partner, and he can speak for you. You trust one another; you're building a life together; and it is that same life that begins to take on its own momentum. You're overwhelmed at work; he isn't getting the attention he wants or needs. This can be a vulnerable stage in the relationship. How do you respond consciously to his and your own dissatisfaction and discontent? Contain.

It's in the words themselves: Within *woman* is *man*, within *female* is *male*. Surround him with your awareness, contain him in your auric field, build his trust in you by not judging or nagging or questioning, but instead by encouraging, uplifting, and elevating.

This won't be easy. You're in the same boat. You're overwhelmed, too; you're exhausted, disappointed, and discontent, too; you need support, too. But at this particular crossroad, you'll need to be the strong one. You'll need to be steady. How can you manifest this kind of inner strength? You'll need to have established a profound inner security that comes only from your relationship to Infinity.

So often, we wrongly place our security in our partner. But this only adds to the pressure. If instead, you can call upon Infinity to cover you and contain you during these challenging times, you will give your partner the room he needs to relax and breathe, and finally, to recover his sense of Self. In this way, you give your partner the opportunity to return to himself—and to you—without any shame or blame; you will have successfully contained your partner and covered him at a time when he needed it most. You'll always be a champion in his mind and heart for having served him in this way.

 *Mold*

The notion that a woman can change her man is fraught with all kinds of controversy. But in fact, a woman changes a man simply by her presence; there's no getting out of it. Every woman, if she's honest with herself, will admit that there are some things that she'd like to change. In ways both big and small, a woman adjusts, nudges, cajoles, and generally makes every effort to shape her man into the ideal. It's a sign of love, but it can also be perceived as "nagging." How do you mold your man into his highest Self? Well, the answer lies in the question. It can only work if you mold your man into the highest expression of himself, not the highest expression of your desires. You don't get to mold your partner into what you want. This is the mistake most women make. They have an idea of who they want their partner to be (men do this, too!), and then they spend the majority of the relationship not relating to who they're with but trying to shape and mold them into who they wanted to be with.

Your creative power is at its most profound here, in the molding and shaping of your environments, your family, and your man. How are you most effective? Through your prayer, your projection. Words won't make the difference; pushing won't affect the change; but your prayer, the prayer of the beloved, can change the destiny. Compassion, love, and patience—lots of it—will also help. There is a prayer called *Sopurkh*[24] that is said to deliver God in the form of man. This prayer, combined with your projection, can mean the difference between living with a man and living with the Divine.

 *Preserve*

Here's where your mettle will truly be tested. Is your commitment ready to stand up to the toughest, most challenging questions to arise in any marriage or long-term relationship? Infidelity. Deceit. Estrangement. Depression. Disease. Injury. Aging. Are you willing to work to preserve the relationship? Is it a shared value? Can you continue to relate to each other honestly, in integrity? Can you practice compassion in the face of devastating loss or betrayal? Can you forgive? Can you find your way home to each other again?

Preserving the commitment in the face of such hardship is very rarely valued any more. Most people want to cut their losses and move on. In a way, this is a relationship's way of coming full circle. But instead of being tempered by fire, this is a journey through the philosopher's stone, where gross metals are transformed into gold. In the beginning, you tested each other's willingness to stay

---

24 This prayer is found in *Rehiras*, the evening prayer of the Sikhs. See *I AM A WOMAN: Essential Kriyas for Women in the Aquarian Age* (Santa Cruz, NM: Kundalini Research Institute, 2009) for more information.

because you had been abandoned in the past. Now you test each other's willingness to stay because you want to know, "Will you love me no matter what?" You ask this of your partner because you cannot ask it of yourself. If you come to this crossroad in your relationship, and you most likely will, don't despair. It's a profound opportunity to heal—to heal your beloved and, in the process, heal yourself. If you ask those who have come to this crossroad and chosen to preserve the relationship over ending it, most will say they are grateful they made it to the other side—still holding their beloved's hand. That is grace.

Harmonious relationships, peaceful, loving homes, and cozy environments—these are the things we all hope for. Meditate on these principles. Practice them. Cultivate a constant and consistent relationship with your own soul. Deepen your understanding of your Self and always listen with your intuition. This is the key to harmony and happiness. This is your birthright, your gift, and your grace.

Chapter Seven

The Art of Creativity

The Divine Mother

Woman is the creative energy, woman is the beauty, woman is the grace, woman is the primal energy which creates the human being.[25]

—*Yogi Bhajan*

Here in northern New Mexico, we are surrounded by images of the Divine Mother. Around every corner you can find the image of the Virgen de Guadalupe, La Reina de Mexico, evidence of the long history of Catholicism in New Mexico, but also of the deeper roots of the Native peoples who have lived here for generations upon generations—the Beauty Way of the Hopi and the Navajo. Native peoples here have a long tradition of living communally, supporting

25 © The Teachings of Yogi Bhajan, August 12, 1978

themselves through an agrarian, sustainable culture—the ancient pueblo. They were matriarchal and matrilineal cultures long before the Spanish or the English arrived. The land here resonates and reflects the healing, creative capacity of the woman and her sustained energy in building and protecting an egalitarian society, both in the home and in the community, generation after generation.

This land and its people are imbued with the qualities of the Divine Mother; it mirrors her grace, reflects her generosity, and unfolds her breathtaking beauty at every turn. It makes sense that Yogi Bhajan came here to begin what he called the Grace of God Movement, in order to show women the nature of our creativity and its double-edged sword. Women can create heaven or hell. We can create prosperity, or we can strip the world bare. Look at Mother Nature—her fecundity and seemingly endless abundance in contrast with her capacity for absolute destruction. These same qualities lie in the woman. If you don't accept both sides of your nature, then you can never act from consciousness and create the world you long for—a world of peace.

So what does it mean to act from consciousness? It means that you not only acknowledge your creativity but also take responsibility for it and its outcomes. It means you act from intention, you honor your word, and you live in integrity. You are creative; your word, your touch, your gaze—all create outcomes. It's in your nature. What does this mean in your day-to-day life? Well, it means that there are no off-the-record statements or moments; there's no time when you're not "on." Does this mean you can't have fun anymore? Of course not. Does it mean you'll never make a mistake? Absolutely not. But it does mean that with each breath, you become more and more awake to your creative potential. It means that with every breath, you understand your vastness and your capacity to create hope. It means that with every breath, you generate just a little more kindness, a little more compassion, a little more tenderness in your own life and in the world around you.

A woman's nature is to nurture. Like the earth, she takes a seed and gives it a home—a place to unfold. And here is the key: A woman, in her most elevated, creative state, allows the other to become itself—nothing more and nothing less. She provides the projection and the prayer, the guidance and the strength, the freedom and the space for the seed to be; and in that being, the seed has an opportunity to become the best. Much of a woman's life is spent nurturing another's seed—her husband's, her children's, her work. Yet at her most exquisite, the seed, the flower, and the fruit are her own.

I remember a conversation with my mother a few years ago. I was making amends, and in that amends, I mentioned that what I most admired about her was this: Everything she touched expressed her artistry. She was indeed an artist, and not the "technician" she had always feigned to be. I, of course, had no idea at the time how important that simple acknowledgment would be to her, but it was everything. She cried and said very simply, "I thought no one ever noticed." And in that moment, I saw how crucial the creativity of a woman is to her life. It informs everything she does, from the smallest flower arrangement, to the most delicate pastry, to the most subtle combination of words, to the most forward-thinking business plan, to the most balanced equation, to the most exquisitely written code. A woman's creativity is the key to her vitality, her endurance, and her strength. It is her grace.

But this key only works when it's opening the door, when it's allowing the flow, when it's nurturing the natural unfolding. If the key is used to turn the lock, then everything that is good and productive in a woman's nature abruptly turns toward destruction.

That same projection and prayer are now corrupt and controlling, that same guidance and strength are now manipulative and smothering, and what was freedom and space become distorted into a kind of prison. These too are the fruits of our creativity—if we're not careful, if we're not conscious.

Conscious Pregnancy[26]

I believe it takes only one woman and one birth to change the whole planet. All it takes is one woman to create one consciousness equal to Guru Nanak or Christ or Buddha. Guru Nanak came out of a woman. Jesus came out of Mary; Krishna, Buddha, everybody, including me, came out of a woman. Therefore, I honestly believe that it is the glory of the woman that spreads the light on this earth.[27]

A woman's most obvious expression of her creativity is in childbirth. It has become popular in today's culture to hear, "Any man can father a child, but not every man can become a father." The same is true of women. Of course, modern medicine has made it much easier for a woman to plan her pregnancies; but even with the relief that contraception has brought to generations of women, those same medical advances have introduced an entirely new set of questions for the modern family. And yes, mistakes still happen; people are still human. Most of these questions, and the answers that women come to, are entirely private. But it's important to address destruction as an act of creativity, too.

The yogic teachings speak of the soul entering the womb at 120 days of gestation. Until that point, the woman has a choice—become a mother or not. She must ask herself some very important questions:

---

26 Pregnancy and mothering is a vast topic covered by The Teachings of Yogi Bhajan. For more information, see *Conscious Pregnancy* by Tarn Taran Kaur Khalsa, available at www.kundaliniwomen.org.
27 © The Teachings of Yogi Bhajan, July 6, 1979 and July 9, 1981

"Am I prepared—mentally, financially, and emotionally—to give this child everything it could possibly need? Am I ready to sacrifice my life to this soul's destiny? Can I provide the environments and conditions that will allow this soul to unfold? Can I produce the prayer that will create not just a good person, but a saint?" For those women who find themselves pregnant under idyllic conditions, these questions may be met with some reluctance, self-doubt, or even surprise, but generally any insecurities or questions are met with a resounding yes. For those who find themselves pregnant under less than idyllic circumstances, however, the answer is sometimes no. Two wrongs do not make a right.

For those women who can't say yes, it's often best to end the pregnancy before the first 120 days is completed, before the soul has entered the womb and contracted with its destiny. If the pregnancy is ended before the 120th day, the yogic teachings indicate that there is no karma. Up to that point, she's not a mother—yet. As a woman, the choice is still available to her: become a mother or not. Whether this decision on the woman's part is selfish or unselfish is not a moral judgment I'm willing to make; but I will say for myself, it is a conscious decision, a deliberate decision, a painful decision. And in its way, it is a grace—even when it may not feel like it at the time.

My own story is the story of no. I was young, but not too young. I was even engaged to be married. But in that moment, sitting on the edge of the toilet and looking into a plastic wand that would determine my future, I realized that I wasn't ready to be a mother. In fact, I realized that the man I had just moments ago been ready to spend my life with was not the man I wanted to be the father of my children. He was still a child himself. It was a rude awakening. I had always been pro-choice; even with my conservative background, I believed in a woman's right to choose from the moment I could make such decisions for myself. I would defend it for others, but of course I never imagined myself having to make that choice. And in reality, I don't know that I made it; it was simply something I knew, immediately, deep in my bones, in that cramped attic apartment, on that hot summer day. I wasn't ready to be a mom. I wasn't ready to make those sacrifices. I didn't trust my fiancé to be my husband or to be this child's father. The dream I had been living quickly became reality—and that reality wasn't what I wanted.

Combining that sudden realization with other factors—I was still in college, I was ashamed to tell my family, and I was quickly becoming an addict—I made a decision that I've never regretted since, but that at the time was the hardest thing I had ever done. Some would suggest that in saying no, I defined myself, by that one act, as a bad mother. I can't say; and now, at age 41, I have often wondered if that was my only chance. But in the years following that pivotal decision in my life, I've consistently found that it was the right one. If you're not ready to welcome that soul, then the child is already compromised—before she's even born. Yogi Bhajan famously said, "God didn't say go forth and create neurotics!" I've since reconciled myself to my life as it is today. Because in the end, there's a reason I said no. There's a reason I've never had children—and in fact, never married. What I can say is this: There's often no right or wrong decisions. There's only the experience and the pain and the growth—and it's all grace.

For those women who say, "Yes, I'm ready to become a mother," those first 120 days can be the most poignant, prayerful days of the pregnancy. Becoming a mother is a sacred trust, and in these first few months of pregnancy, she has the opportunity to call to herself a soul of great caliber, a soul who will be a blessing to the world, a soul that will become known as a gift. This is the first act of mothering—calling out to a child. Reaching toward that shared destiny and saying yes. It's crucial for a woman during these first 120 days to meditate, and in that meditation, that stillness, to cultivate a consciousness of peace, harmony, and happiness. Meditating in this way acts like a beacon to draw toward her a soul that matches her vibration, her consciousness, and her grace.

On the 120th day, the soul enters the womb, and the contract is completed. That mother and child are now bound together. In many ways, the remaining days of the pregnancy determine the child's destiny; for it is in these final weeks and months in the womb that the mother's prayer can change the child's destiny and imprint it with the *naam*—the vibration of Infinity. Yogi Bhajan often said that saints are made because of their mother's prayer. Jesus, Mohammed, Buddha, Nanak are all products of their mother's prayer, their mother's devotion, their mother's kindness.

Imagine if every woman approached her pregnancy and her parenting in this way, with total devotion, projection, and prayer, dedicating her child's life to peace. Within one generation, our world will have transformed. Imagine if the mothers of Gaza and the mothers of Israel decided to teach their children to love each other, rather than hate. Imagine if they instilled in their children the values of tolerance, forgiveness, and acceptance. Imagine if we, as Americans, taught our children the virtues of nonviolence and the dangers of nuclear proliferation. We could raise a generation of leaders who would finally realize the goal of Global Zero—a world free of nuclear weapons, now and forever. Imagine a generation of women who raised their sons to honor not only their mothers, but every woman, as their sister, their auntie, or their daughter.

Grace Note

Meditate on this prayer and see your child as the Infinite reflection of God:

Remembering God, all shortcomings depart and one's generations are saved. Meditate continually on the Lord, who has no end or limit. O child, this is your mother's hope and prayer, that you may never forget the Lord, even for an instant. May you ever vibrate upon the Lord of the Universe. May the True Guru be kind to you, and may you  *love the Society of the Saints. May the preservation of your honor through the Lord's grace be your clothing, and may the singing of His Praises be your food. Forever drink the Ambrosial Nectar; and may you live long, and may the meditative remembrance of the Lord give you infinite delight. May joy and pleasure be yours; may your hopes be fulfilled, and may you never be troubled by worries. Let this mind of yours be the bumble bee, and let the Lord's feet be the lotus flower. Attach your mind to the Lord's feet, and blossom forth like the songbird, upon finding the raindrop.*

—Guru Arjan, a 16th-century saint

After meditating on this prayer for several days, write your own prayer and recite it every day for your child. This is the mother's grace.

Imagine the transformation in our culture if women were no longer exploited or made into commodities or subjected to violence. The prayer of the mother, the consciousness of the mother, can begin to turn the tide and change the destiny of an entire generation. Be that mother; become that grace.

Several technologies in the Kundalini Yoga tradition support the mother's prayer and a conscious pregnancy. As a community, we welcome the child's soul on the 120th day with a celebration and chanting; then we meditate upon that soul throughout the pregnancy, and sustain and protect the child throughout its life with continued chanting and prayer. Of these practices, there is one that can be incorporated at any time and will bless a mother and her child throughout their journey together.

Yogi Bhajan says that "bearing a child is not a human job; bearing a child is a totally divine, divine, divine job. From the 120th day to the day of delivery, whatever you put in through prayer is going to come out."[28] The prayer of the mother is the most powerful thing in the Universe. A mother's prayer has the power to rewrite destiny. Many of the metaphors in the following practice may not mean much to you now, because they reflect the traditional gifts in the Eastern tradition. But upon meditation and reflection, they will grow in significance. The longing reflected in this prayer is really beautiful if you understand its origin. For example, the songbird and the raindrop: There is a bird in India that drinks only when water falls as rain; so the raindrop is very precious and longed for. So, too, is the soul's longing for God, for divinity, and for infinity in one's life.

In addition to prayer and meditation, a mother's physical preparation will also serve both her and her child. What she eats, what she surrounds herself with, her environments, and how she

28 © The Teachings of Yogi Bhajan, circa 1977

prepares her body and mind for the birth will make a big difference in the overall experience. If you are a soon-to-be-mother, prepare your body through daily walking (up to 5 miles a day) and yoga asanas; for the hips and lower back, incorporate cat-cow, butterfly, and squats every day; for your upper back and breasts, try spine flex, twists, and shoulder shrugs.[29] Prepare your mind not only through meditation but also with a thoughtful birth plan. Know what you want going in—and have a support group to affirm and confirm that plan throughout any and all contingencies. Consciously relax every day, consciously breathe every day, and consciously move every day; this will prepare your mind and your body for the discipline of labor and the grace of mothering.

The First 40 Days & Beyond

Once the child is born, the intuition and sensitivity of the mother only increase—along with exhaustion and sleepless nights. For the first 40 days, it's best if the mother and child remain in seclusion. Friends and family can visit, but it's crucial to support and protect the child's and the mother's auras during this most vulnerable time. The mother needs to rest, and the child needs to nurse in a relaxed and supportive environment; no outside stressors should be introduced, if at all possible. These 40 days should be spent bonding, cuddling, singing, meditating, and walking. A mother living in rhythm with her child and with her own cycles will allow the child to establish her own rhythm, which in time will begin to reflect the mother's. This rhythm is so important in establishing security for a child. The more experiences she can begin to predict, the more secure and relaxed she will be.

---

29 See Everyday Asanas on page 160

The Teachings of Yogi Bhajan include many simple techniques that strengthen the child's nervous system, support the aura of the mother and child, and help renew the mother's strength after giving birth. His teachings also include techniques that support the child's physical and spiritual growth and maturity. Here are a few simple practices:

A newborn infant is much more comfortable and at ease when she's in your arms. But when you're ready to lay her down—for example, after nursing—she will rest more deeply when bundled. Imagine coming out of this tiny, dark, cozy, warm space into a bright, cold, sterile world. To support her nervous system, bundle (or swaddle) her tightly in a warm, flannel cotton blanket. She'll relax and end up sleeping more deeply and for longer periods of time.

Two more techniques that strengthen the newborn's nervous system are infant massage and cold dips. First, massage the child with cold-pressed almond oil in long strokes along the arms, legs, and spine and in light clockwise circles on the belly. After this light massage, dip your child in cold water two or three times. Then dry her off and bundle her up. The combination of the cold water and the warming massage will tone your child's nervous system and strengthen her reflexes.

As a new mother, following a few simple rules will support not only your child but also your recovery. Sleep when the baby sleeps! This is crucial for you to get enough rest in the first few weeks and months after your child's birth. Also, having the child sleep in the same bed or in an adjacent bed to yours will ease nighttime feedings and will keep the child in your aura, ensuring her security and comfort. This same technique also helps during the day. Rather than using a stroller, try carrying your child against you when you're out and about, at least for the first few weeks. For your own health and well-being, introduce blackstrap molasses, brewer's yeast, and Golden Milk[30], a combination of milk, turmeric and oil, into your diet to support your mineral balance and to reduce inflammation after the birth.

Beyond those first 40 days, the child's first three years are crucial for her development. As explained earlier, as the mother, you are your child's first teacher. The values and virtues that you instill in your child, by your example and through your guidance and prayer, lay the foundation for who that child later becomes. This isn't to say a child isn't responsible for her own life; rather it is to reinforce the powerful influence of the mother—positively or negatively. A mother can make of her child a saint—or not.

All that a child gains or suffers comes from how the mother speaks to him or her. Always speak angelically to the child. Out of that is born the divinity, the dignity, the grace, the future, the destiny, the fate, the luck, and the prosperity of the child. If you do not recognize your own child as an angel, you'll never recognize your child.[31]

As a woman, you have the capacity to create a saint who can be a light to the world, a harbinger of peace, a servant of the poor and dispossessed, a gift to humanity. Every child is a mirror of his or her mother, just as the world is a mirror of us all. This can be a terrifying prospect for the new mother. I remember my sister calling and saying, "If I had known it would be this hard to see myself in my children, I don't know that I could have done it." She, of course, has since grown to appreciate the mirror that her children have become for her—and she has grown stronger and better because of them. (And yes, they are all saints! But then again, I am their aunt, and so a bit prejudiced in my opinions.) In all

---

30 See Everyday Recipes on page 156.
31 © The Teachings of Yogi Bhajan, June 29, 1989

seriousness, I can see the good that is in my sister made manifest in her children. They are noble, serviceful, radiant, intelligent human beings who bring light and joy wherever they go. So my sister has fulfilled her destiny as a mother—she has given the world the gift of leadership, love, music, poetry, devotion, and more.

Remembering the communication principles of the graceful woman—innocence, radiance, and directness—and applying them to how you speak to your children will go a long way toward developing their sense of independence, self-respect, and tolerance. They'll have an opportunity to become themselves and not simply an extension of you, their mother. This is the greatest gift any mother can give to her child—an opportunity to meet his or her destiny and fulfill it.

Creativity & the Woman

Beyond her role as mother, a woman's creativity is infinite—and the world is a mirror of that creativity. Applied to the arts, politics, cooking, gardening, teachings, business, or the sciences, a woman's capacity to nurture and nurse things into being is her gift, not only to her field but also to the world—and to her Self. A woman needs to be creative in order to have a sense of purpose. Her sense of identity must always dwell in the realm of infinity. If a woman begins to feel trapped by any single role or identity, she begins to shut down and becomes vulnerable to depression and behaviors driven by subconscious agendas that don't serve her identity or her Infinity. Her creative, expansive capacity must always be in the flow. Otherwise, the stagnation, boredom, and feelings of uselessness will overwhelm her.

Grace Note

Return to the symbol of the Adi Shakti—your infinite creativity. Raise your arms above your head, making a graceful arc. Roll your eyes up and feel the space between your hands. Now, from your tailbone to the crown of your head, project into that space everything you want to create. Project your identity, your creativity, your vision, and your manifestation.

As you pull up from the tailbone, the First Chakra, experience the energy moving through every part of your spine and merge that energy with your projection. From your tailbone, bring in the resources and the foundation you need to begin. From your Second Chakra, your sexual organs, add the juice and the flow you need to move the projection along. From your Third Chakra, the Navel Point, add fire—the energy and the catalyst to launch your projection into being. From the Fourth Chakra, the Heart Center, add the element of wind to sustain the fire's growth. Blend in your kindness and compassion, too, so that your projection serves others as well as your Self. From the Fifth Chakra, the throat, add refinement and subtly, along with the directness you may need to hurdle any final obstacles. From the Sixth Chakra, the Third Eye, bring in insight and intuition. Meditate on your vision. From the Seventh Chakra, the Crown, expand your vision into your radiance, unto Infinity. Give it to the universe so that the universe can deliver it. Feel all that energy come into the space between your hands; know it to be real. Breathe deeply; experience your Infinity. To seal the practice, inhale deeply, suspend the breath, and hold your vision. Exhale completely and relax your arms. Sit quietly and trust that everything your heart desires will unfold.

Women are twice as likely to experience depression as men.[32] Multiple factors contribute, including unequal power and status, sexual and physical abuse, and overload at work and in the home. The gender differences that coincide with puberty and menopause indicate that hormonal shifts are another major contributor to depression in women. These factors cannot be underestimated, and yet so much of a woman's identity is more than her chemical makeup or her social background. Much of a woman's depression lies in her lack of self-fulfillment through creativity. Although parenting is one of the most sacred acts any one of us can do, it's still not enough for most. A woman's key to happiness is her creativity—not her family, her husband, her children, or even her work. These relationships bring joy, but they aren't what fills a woman; that can only come from herself and her creativity. A woman's infinite creativity demands more of herself and her experience of the world.

A woman's creativity can be fulfilled in ways both large and small. The story of my own mother shows how she has brought her creativity and artistry to everything she has touched: her home, her garden, her animals, her knitting projects, her reading and study. Everything she has contributed to or participated in has allowed her to express her creativity. So, too, every woman must find her medium of expression. Maybe it's cooking. Maybe it's writing. Maybe it's dancing. Maybe it's singing. Maybe it's service. Find that thing—or those myriad things—that fulfill you, that make you come alive. Experience your life at its fullest. That is your grace.

32 Research on depression and women from the Mayo Clinic (www.mayoclinic.com).

Chapter Eight

The Art of Healing

The Touch of Grace

You want to be able to touch and heal everything—that is your mother instinct.[33]

—*Yogi Bhajan*

How do we change yesterday? We do so by changing the story. Whatever our story, we can change it simply by practicing forgiveness. Forgive. Why should we forgive? What should we "give for"? For ourselves! Forgiveness is the only way out of our own misery—self-inflicted or not. Through forgiveness, we get to rewrite the story. What was once festering and dark is brought into the light of day; and through our own applied consciousness, we give ourselves the opportunity to own the story—instead of having the story own us. Imagine the women and men of South Africa in

33 © The Teachings of Yogi Bhajan, Summer 1982

the Truth and Reconciliation hearings describing the murder of their children or their experiences of rape and violence. Imagine the power they reclaimed by telling their story. So, too, imagine the forgiveness, the cleansing, that the perpetrators experienced as they recounted the horrors enacted by their own hands.

Anything we bring out into the light of day loses its power. Just as a nightlight drove away all our childhood terrors, so the light of consciousness shines on those dark places within our psyche. All those old wounds that were once great obstacles now become our way out—our guideposts on the healing journey of the Self. Accountability and forgiveness go hand in hand toward healing the patterns that hold us back from fulfilling our truest destiny—living healthy, happy, and holy lives and building a world of peace.

But the peace we seek out there, in the world, must begin at home, within our Self and our families. How much self-loathing do you still heap upon yourself each and every day? How much false bravado do you generate through mindless affirmations? How often do you experience frustration—or even rage—at your own children or your partner? The kind of healing we need can't come if we continue to beat ourselves up; nor can it come on the heels of New Age positive thinking. It only arrives when we drop the past, live in the present, and align our will to our actions. Self-integrity is the most profound manifestation of healing, but it's hard won. It begins with a decision, a commitment: "Today I'm going to be kind to myself. Today I'm going to practice forgiveness—toward myself and others. Today I'm going to do what I say I will do." These three simple practices can open the door to a profound new way of being in the world.

Don't get me wrong—this isn't easy! In fact, it's probably the hardest thing any of us will ever try to do. Our culture makes it easy to continue to be negative about ourselves—our looks, our performance in bed, our children's behavior. You name it, there's something for you to feel bad about! So practicing kindness toward ourselves and others is a profound act of self-integrity. Kindness is akin to healing. A thoughtful word, a small deed, a gentle touch are all healing, especially to the Self. Giving to others in this way can profoundly transform our own experience in the world. These simple acts of service remove any sense of isolation and stimulate the pleasure centers in the brain. Kindness feels good—and don't we all want to feel good. That's, in a sense, the definition of *health*: "I feel good."

So, too, forgiveness is a radical departure from our culture's narrative of shame and blame—it, too, is a form of kindness. In one traditional prayer, known as the *ardas*, there is a line that says, "Let us see the faults of others and overlook them." So the act of forgiveness doesn't arise from blindness or naivety, but rather from a clear-sighted knowing and then the decision to forgive, to overlook, to relate to their highest nature. Imagine doing this for ourselves. Not denying our faults or sublimating them in some way, but instead seeing them with clear-eyed objectivity and then letting them go. Forgiving ourselves, choosing not to define ourselves by our weaknesses but, instead, by our strengths, our core identity—this goes a long way toward profound healing of the Self and reunion with the soul's purpose.

The final step toward self-integrity? Living your word. As we discussed in Chapter Five, as women, our word is one of the most profound tools for change and transformation we have, but only if it is applied consciously and with integrity. What does this mean on a daily basis? We must begin with a simple commitment to do those things we say we'll do. In a world of fad dieting, resolutions, and overscheduling, this can be extraordinarily challenging. How often have we said to ourselves, "I'm going to start tomorrow"? How often have we said one thing only to find ourselves doing just the opposite minutes or days later? How often have we made a promise to someone and then had to back out because we didn't have the time? Each of these circumstances is a call to keeping our word. In each case, we have to profoundly commit our entire Self to our word; we have to align our actions to our will. It's harder than it sounds. For addicts, it's close to impossible. But if we have the capacity to be honest, then we have the capacity to marshal our actions and our will into agreement.

In the words of one great master, we "agree to agree."[34] We say yes. We follow through. This, too, is a profound healing. Imagine how much emotional and mental energy we would each save simply by doing what we say we'll do. No more berating ourselves; no more beating ourselves up; no more disappointing other people. As we master this newfound self-integrity, our boundaries become healthier and stronger; we engender trust; people begin to count on us as we drop years of negative habits and feelings of shame, and instead experience a newfound energy and vitality to deliver on our destiny. Basically we grow up.

As important as it is for each of us to experience this inner healing and to practice kindness, forgiveness, and integrity, it's equally important to return these values to our culture. But how? Not to be overly sentimental about the past, but it often seems that as a culture, we've lost touch with the most basic forms of civility in many areas of life: communication, transportation, politics, religion, and more. It's one thing to be kind to the person next to you, to even forgive that person, and to have that kindness

34 The *Mann-ai Pauris*, found in *Japji Sahib*, by the 15th-century saint Guru Nanak Dev Ji

and forgiveness create a wave of action and reaction that changes things. It's quite another to return kindness and forgiveness back to the public discourse and sphere of action, to make it a part of the social system again. And integrity and ethics are an entirely different ballpark!

Political figures have begun to turn the tide and recognize that you can disagree without being disagreeable. Schools are beginning to implement communication trainings so bullies no longer benefit from their bullying. And yet, as I write this chapter, a young woman was gang-raped as a crowd stood by and watched. How can this be? How is it possible? Perhaps the greatest healing we can affect on the world is to never allow something like this to happen again. But then we say that every time it happens—and it happens every day, in ways both large and small. From the Central Park jogger who cried for help to the young woman on the corner trading her flesh for money to the addict who sleeps behind the trash bin—all these people are crying for help, literally or figuratively. So why are we so afraid to be kind to them? What holds us back from becoming involved?

I lived in Seattle, Washington for many years. I would often see people passed out behind the corner market, or tripping as they walked downtown, or smelling of urine and decay while riding the bus. And I looked away. Most of us look away. The one time I didn't look away, I found a friend. Andrew was homeless and schizophrenic; but when he was well, he was brilliant and creative—a true artist. When he wasn't well, he was terrifying, and it was confusing and painful to witness. I don't have any profound conclusions, but I know for myself that I was afraid to feel the pain, as if it were a contagion. But even as I admit my fear of extending myself to another, I also know that as a recovered addict,

Grace Note

Tune in and then sit with your hands at your Heart Center, left hand resting on the heart, right hand resting over the left. The hands make an X at the Heart Center. Close your eyes and sit straight and relaxed. Become fully present. Begin to focus on the Heart Center, the Hirday Chakra, the seat of the heartbeat. Feel your heart beating; this is the rhythm of your life. Imagine that you are hypnotizing yourself. Become aware, alert, present, and relaxed. Bring all of your attention to a single, tiny ray of light that is circling you. This ray is a very bright, distinct, white, shining, platinum light; a circling ray that moves incredibly fast and smooth around your body. Now make it two rays. Three. Four. Now a multitude of rays surround your entire being. Imagine a ray of light for every one of your ten trillion cells! You are a light, swirling and communicating between every cell, each with its own intelligence. The rays are moving faster and faster, infinitely fast. Keep imagining deeper, and deeper, and deeper. Sustain this imagery. This is Wahe Guru, the ecstasy of knowing the Divine, in every molecule, in every atom of you. This is the exact imagery of the mantra Ang Sang Wahe Guru,[1] "my every cell vibrates with the ecstasy of the Divine Naam." To end the meditation, chant the mantra, Ang Sang Wahe Guru, for several minutes—until you experience that vibration throughout your entire body.

1 From the meditation, Healing Imagery, © The Teachings of Yogi Bhajan, July 5, 1991. *Ang Sang* is pronounced like *hung* in English. *Wa* is a long 'a' like water; *he* is pronounced like *hay*. **Guru** has a short and a long 'u' sound, *uh* and *oo*, respectively: *guroo*.

one simple act of kindness from a stranger was what allowed me to stay sober that first day. And that day became two, and those days became weeks, and weeks became years, and I celebrated 10 years of sobriety this year. To practice kindness, then, we must profoundly heal ourselves and our fears and act from our connection to Infinity,

because Infinity is what allows us to expand, to become fearless, and to be kind, which is a healing to others and ourselves.

As a woman, both Shakti and Bhakti—power and devotion—dwell within every cell of your body. That power can heal you, your family, your lineage—and the world. That devotion calls you to serve, to touch, and to give. Kindness and compassion are your grace; courage and clarity, your clarion call. To merge and manifest these qualities within you, within your human body,

Grace Note

Come back to that space—that swirling being of light—and breathe deeply. Sit with your hands in front of your shoulders, palms out. Feel the space. Begin to tune in to the palms of your hands, the tips of your fingers, the surface of your skin, the quality of the air. Close your eyes and feel the space; tune in to the energy and bring that energy into your hands with your breath. Breathe deeply and slowly. Imagine that you're breathing through the palms of your hands. Feel the prana, the life force, coming into your body, into every cell—Ang Sang Wahe Guru—every limb, every finger. Tune in to the sound of your breath, sohung, "I am that". I am the breath. I am the breath of life. Listen to the sound of your own breath. Now begin to make the sound "ah." Inhale deeply; exhale as you chant the sound and feel the space. Experience the flow of prana; the movement of light and air and sound. After several minutes of charging your hands in this way, bring them to your body. Touch your heart, your neck, or your knees—some place that's achy or uncomfortable. Continue to create the sound. Continue to breathe deeply and slowly. Continue to bring the prana into the center of your palms and send that energy into your body. Notice the shift. This is a healing. This is your grace.

you must realize the light and the music that dance within every cell of your body. In our tradition, this dance is called *Ang Sang Wahe Guru*, which simply means "every cell of my body vibrates with the ecstasy of being brought from darkness to light." What follows is a simple healing meditation that calls in the light and the music that move with every beat of your heart. Realize this healing within yourself, so that you can, in turn, heal others. Command the elements, command your world—this is your grace.

This vibration, this light, is your radiance. Yogi Bhajan often said that the simplest, purist way to serve is with our presence. Our presence should be a healing. Imagine that idea for a moment. Imagine that when you enter a room, people experience relief, people feel better, even though they don't know why. That's the goal. That's the purpose. That is grace. There is a tree in India called the Remover of Sorrows, and it is said that meditating beneath that tree can heal you of any dis-ease, sadness, or depression. Imagine your every breath, your every word, your every touch becoming a remover of sorrows. Imagine the canopy of your own radiance delivering that kind of healing, that quality of comfort, that depth of succor, that level of protection. This vibration, this quality of light and radiance is experienced through your touch. That touch is a healing.

I grew up in a family where my father was a doctor. But sometimes when I was sick, I just wanted my mom to come in and be with me, give me some orange juice, rub my back, and make me feel better. That's the healing power of a mother's touch; so much so that the child longs for it. Every woman has this power to heal through her touch. With your breath, your prayer, your intention, and your meditation, you can charge your hands consciously and use them to bless yourself and others.

You can use this same technique on your family and friends, bringing comfort and ease just through your touch.

Another way to bring this kind of healing, this kind of touch, and this way of being into your day is through relaxation. We live in a 24-7 culture. There's always something to do, somewhere to go, someone to see. Once upon a time, there were blue laws, which meant that on Sunday's in the South, everything was closed. You had to rest, because there was nothing else to do. Religious traditions set aside a day to relax and restore—the Sabbath—or a season to turn inward and focus on prayer and fasting—Ramadan and Lent. And yet most of our culture has lost touch with these traditions. Many of us don't even know how to relax anymore.

Leisure time in contemporary culture is filled with television or online games or searching the Web or checking our BlackBerry®. We're inundated with information, stimulation, all day long. This constant "on" mode, this state of being on-the-go, creates a state of tension in the body that's never given the opportunity to "stand down." Chemically, our tissues become filled with cortisol and adrenaline, and we begin to experience pain in our muscles and joints. Emotionally, we begin to experience stress and fear—and we often don't know why. Instead we sense an undifferentiated anxiety that only creates more confusion. Physically, our breath becomes shorter and shallower, which, in turn, creates more of those same symptoms—undifferentiated anxiety, physical pain, and hormonal imbalances.

So how do you create a new normal for yourself and your surroundings? How do you consciously relax throughout your day? How do you bring that conscious relaxation to others in your life? Practicing awareness and bringing that awareness into every part of your day will serve you in learning to consciously relax. Begin playing meditative, relaxing music in the background: in your home, at your workplace, while you drive. Learn to stop and take a breath when you're upset or uneasy. This small step, taken throughout the day, will do wonders to bring relaxation and healing into your daily life.

Grace Note

Incorporate the following exercise into your daily routine. Set the alarm on your phone to go off once each hour. Bring your hands to your belly, close your eyes, and breathe deeply: three deep breaths. Then open your eyes, smile, and continue on with your day. Practice this every day, until it becomes a habit and you no longer need the alarm.

Another simple tool that has helped me so much since I began using it in my daily routine is the *mala*. I'm generally an easily agitated person. Fiery by nature, I'm quick to anger, but also quick to laugh. Sitting in meetings used to be really challenging for me, until a beloved friend gave me a mala for my 40th birthday. Since then, I bring out my mala any time I need to slow down, practice patience, or simply be still: meetings, waiting rooms, and sometimes even my car if I'm stuck in traffic. A practice that's found in almost every religious tradition, the mala allows your mind to attune itself to a constant rhythm and motion, even when all around you may be generating agitation, boredom, or stress. Known alternately as worry beads, prayer beads, rosary beads, or meditation beads, a mala is a tool to elevate your consciousness that can be applied to any situation. Simply run the beads along your fingers and silently vibrate your highest identity with each bead: love, truth, peace, Sat Nam, Wahe Guru—whatever vibration brings you the internal alignment necessary to be your highest Self in any given moment. Malas can be made of anything: seeds, semiprecious stones, metals. There is a great deal of information out there about what qualities each stone or metal brings to the practitioner; do a little research and find a mala that resonates with what you need in order to bring more balance and relaxation into your daily life.

Healing with Food

Another way to bring healing to yourself and those around you is through food. For thousands of years, women have used herbs and healing foods to maintain health and vitality and to heal the body, mind, and emotions. Just the smell of good food can be a healing. Remember your mother's chicken noodle soup or some other childhood favorite? Think about how exhausted you were when you would come home; then imagine the smell of cinnamon and ginger simmering on the stove. Just the smell lifts your spirits, right?

The slow food movement, combined with eating local produce either through consumer-supported agriculture (CSAs) or the local farmers' market, is changing the face of the American diet. The most healing foods are local, whole, seasonal, and made with loving hands! When we eat the foods that grow where we live, we not only limit the carbon footprint we create with every bite, we also take in a bit of the land, water, and sky in which we live, which supports our body and mind in merging and experiencing union with our environments. Whole food means that we eat as close to the original source as we possibly can. We eat whole grains and vegetables, raw fruits, nuts and greens, and fresh, cold-pressed oils. We limit animal products in the diet in order to avoid the buildup of *ama*, which in Ayurvedic medicine refers to heavy, mucous-building qualities in food that affect the body adversely. Instead, we eat lightly of the foods that are in season. Melons, avocado, tomatoes, and lots of raw greens in the summers; pumpkins, sweet potatoes, kale, and other greens in the fall; oranges and dried fruits, whole grains, and root vegetables in the winter for sustenance; and fennel, asparagus, and new onions in the spring. Just as eating locally keeps you in tune with the land, eating in season keeps you tuned in to the flow of nature and the cycle of life.

What your body most needs for healing in any given season naturally grows at that time. For example, in the spring, when allergies begin to trouble you, nettle grows naturally all across the country. Used in soups or taken as a supplement, nettle can help you avoid most allergies. Or in the winter, when you need the warmth of ginger and garlic in your diet, these roots grow profusely. Yogi Bhajan gave countless remedies over the years. Here I will mention just a few that can make your kitchen cupboard a natural medicine cabinet.

In the beginnings of the flu season, boost your immune system by incorporating a lot of ginger, garlic, and onions into your diet. A tonic that includes lots of ginger—and is welcome during the winter seasons—is Yogi Tea.[35] This blend of spices boosts immunity, cleanses the liver, and nourishes the nervous and glandular systems. In addition, you can add astragalus to your soups or teas. Astragalus is a traditional Indian root that makes a powerful tonic to boost energy, immunity, and vitality. Another great tonic for the winter flu season and other lung problems, such as bronchitis or cough, is black pepper tea. Made with whole black peppercorns, ginger, and a splash of pomegranate juice, this tonic supports the lungs in clearing any excess mucous and warms the tissues to encourage healing. I drink this tonic throughout the winter to support clearing my lungs from years of exposure to smoking, which still nags me in the winter months.

For aching joints and muscle pain, try Golden Milk. Turmeric is an excellent, all-around tonic root/herb for women and can be used as a spice in your cooking or as a concentrated food, as in Golden Milk, or as a supplement. Ground flaxseed also supports the tissues of the body, especially in the winter months when you experience dry skin around the elbows, ankles, and heels. In the summer months, cooling foods and herbs can act as tonics as well. Fresh mint and basil add not only flavor but also cooling qualities to your food. Watermelon can be used as a tonic food in the summers to cool the body, along with cucumber, yogurt, and hot peppers. It's counterintuitive, but spicy food in the summer actually works to cool the body by generating sweat!

Finally, the ultimate healing food—besides your own mother's chicken noodle soup—is known as *kitcheri*, or mung beans and

---

35 See Everyday Recipes on page 156.

rice. This stew is cooked until it becomes a mush. Made with onions, ginger, garlic, and other healing vegetables and spices, this stew is a restorative food. Wonderful for people recovering from serious illness, it also works great as a monodiet cleanse for 3 days, 10 days, 40 days, or more. Of course, none of these tonics are cure-alls. Allopathic medicine has its place in your health-care plans, but many of the nagging and seasonal health problems can be addressed simply by tuning in to your body; boosting your immune system as the seasons change, especially spring and fall; avoiding sugar; and eating high-quality, local food in season—all with a dash of loving intention.

The Healing Crisis

We've been living in the self-help age for quite a while now. The past 10 years have proven especially challenging to anyone who's experienced a chronic illness. Misinterpretations abound. The most common example? "If we are the makers of our reality, then people who have cancer must have asked for it in some way." Blaming the victim is very popular, but it only makes things harder for those trying to recover from life-threatening illnesses. The reality of illness and the way it manifests is much more complicated, subtle, and mysterious—it's the healing crisis. And in everyone's life, at one point or another, each of us will experience this crisis. A healing crisis doesn't always entail a physical illness; it can be psychological, emotional, or spiritual. But one thing is guaranteed in any healing crisis, physical or otherwise—we don't get to decide how it ends. We don't get to determine the outcome with our intellect, our reason, our devotion, or even our prayer.

Powerlessness is at the heart of any healing crisis. And as much work as we do on ourselves, clearing our past, cleansing our bodies, disciplining our minds through meditation—all of it means very little in the face of a healing crisis. So, how can your discipline contribute to overcoming a crisis? It can mean that you're fearless in the face of death. It can mean you're able to discipline your mind to overcome pain. It can mean your devotion and faith will give you the courage to live—even when you don't want to anymore. That's how the work you've done will serve you. But the reality of a healing crisis is that it takes you beyond anything your discipline or devotion could ever imagine or prepare you for. Any illusion of control is long gone. At that point, you just have to ride it out. Seek help where you can, lean on the people you love, and continue your disciplines so that when and if you reach the other side, you have the strength to continue on and be able to serve others going through the same thing or something similar.

The tyranny of self-help demands that we learn something from everything that happens to us. But what we learn isn't necessarily what we imagine. We want it to make us stronger; but what if it simply makes us humbler? We want it to make us fearless; but what if it shows us our vulnerability in ways we were blind to? We want it to make us more devoted, more sure in our faith; but what if it just introduces more questions than we had before? The reality is that life is tenacious, and sometimes we have to play catch-up—or simply show up—and realize we don't have all the answers. The healing crisis simply reminds us that we never had all the answers to begin with. But the healing crisis also gives us so much more: empathy, compassion, and enough self-doubt to make us more human. A healing crisis delivers a depth of surrender that we wouldn't have known had we sailed through life with no storms. And surviving the storm delivers us to a purpose and a clarity that we wouldn't have obtained without this particular journey and these particular circumstances. This is the perfect healing. This is grace.

The art of healing is a lifelong journey to the Self and the soul. A woman's gift is to heal—herself, her family, her generation, those who came before, and those who will follow after. Her art is in her touch, her life, her word, and her love. This is her grace—and may you be that grace today and every day.

Chapter Nine

The Art of Community

Peacemaking in the Aquarian Age

To win the world, the only thing you can do in your life is be a kind speaker and a kind listener. Kindness—that's what makes humankind.[36]

—*Yogi Bhajan*

The recent economic downturn has brought about a return to community—small, local economies being built up around farmers' markets, community swaps, and trading for labor and services. The old-fashioned barn raising is back, but it's embodied in urban gardens, child-care co-ops, and regional currencies to encourage local trade. Economic insecurity has two predictable outcomes: reaching out or keeping out. In the coming Aquarian Age, things

36 © The Teachings of Yogi Bhajan, June 30, 1988

will only grow more insecure; so our capacity to reach out and create ties to our neighbors, our community, and our world is crucial to not only surviving but also thriving in the years to come. That old adage, "think globally, act locally," is more applicable now than ever before; and the return of community is a good sign.

Traditional forms of community are dying away—religious identification is at an all-time low, and political party affiliations are fewer than ever before. People no longer want to conform to a form. Independence in thought and action is the primary value; yet even in our independence, there is an understanding of the virtues of community, felicity, and friendship. From knitting circles to sacred circles to multiuse construction projects, people are returning to the values of working, practicing, shopping, and living in the same community. Once again, people understand the importance of knowing their neighbors. Yet still, there is a search for something greater—an awakening of the soul and the spirit— in every facet of life.

Community building comes naturally to women. We understand intuitively the need for cooperation. We tend to negotiate win-win solutions over zero-sum games. We enjoy creating answers that work for everyone. This idea is counter to much of our contemporary culture; but in the Aquarian Age, this kind of problem solving will be the way everyone begins to think and operate. There will be no room for greed or divisiveness; cooperation will be the key to succeeding—locally and globally. Any notion of family, tribe, or nationality—that is, any self-interest—must be weighed with the needs of everyone: "Recognize that the other person is you."[37] This will challenge every woman's natural instinct to protect her own. But there exists in a woman's psyche an expansiveness, a capacity to

37 The first Aquarian Sutra by Yogi Bhajan, Master of Kundalini Yoga.

envelop everyone as her child, her lover, her family, and her nation. It is this quality that will sustain community and build peace in the coming Age.

One of my earliest memories as a child is of a conversation with my mother—it's a feeling more than an exact recall, but it describes a consciousness that I believe most children are born with but that over time is trained out of them. It's also what I believe is becoming known as the Aquarian Consciousness. Children are acutely aware of justice; they have an innate sensibility about what is fair or unfair. My mother and I were talking about why some people had a lot and others had so little and why things weren't different. She began to explain that families take care of each other and described the history of kin and tribe and state loyalties. And I remember thinking, "But why am I more important to her than any other child in the world?" I remember being acutely aware of my privilege— even being ashamed of it. I honestly didn't understand why I would be more important than any other child; it was a shock to me. This sensibility is inherent in the principle of "the other person is you," and it is key toward changing the consciousness in the coming Age.

The art of community lies in being able to balance those personal loyalties and responsibilities with the understanding that another's security is your own. In order for your interests and your family to be secure, then another person's family and interests must also be secure. These same negotiations are seen every day in the sphere of international relations and negotiations over shared resources, security interests, and the expansion of human rights, education, and health care. What's good for you is good for your neighbor; what's good for your neighbor is good for you. There's a shift in consciousness that recognizes this fundamental truth—at a personal and a global level—like never before. The days of "greed is good" are over. As the world grows smaller via technology and because of more and more limited resources, everyone is waking up to the reality that the principles we learned in kindergarten still apply: "Share everything; play fair; don't hit people; put things back where you found them; clean up your own mess; don't take things that aren't yours; say you're sorry when you hurt somebody; wash your hands before you eat; flush; warm cookies and cold milk are good for you; live a balanced life—learn some and think some and draw and paint and sing and dance and play and work every day some; and take a nap every afternoon."[38]

Peanut Hour

One of the simplest approaches to community building begins in a most personal way: women friends gathering together to chat. Affectionately known in some circles as "stitch and bitch," these groups in India are called Peanut Hour. Women from the village gather to have tea and to talk about their day as a way to relax and prepare for the return of their children and their husbands. Every woman needs this kind of community, this circle of women to share experiences, troubles, and pain with. It's a way for women to direct their negative mind—their defenses, their complaints, and their criticisms—in a positive way, so that when they're with their families, they can be uplifting and encouraging. It's also a way for women to protect themselves. In traditional communities, the stories shared at Peanut Hour often translated into action when members of the community would retaliate against an abusive husband or family member, seeking justice on behalf of a friend. In this way, village life came to a natural balance and harmony. In many ways, we've lost that balance. But as pointed to earlier, it's making a comeback.

38 Fulghum, Robert, *All I Really Need to Know I Learned in Kindergarten* (New York: Ivy Books, 1989).

Today, there are countless ways for women to connect with each other online: Facebook® and other social networking sites; targeted support networks, such as aa-intergroup.org, an online community of recovered alcoholics; WeightWatchers.com/community, an online weight-loss support group; or ravelry.com, an online knitting community. But even with all these new resources and new ways to connect and create community, nothing beats that face-to-face interaction with a friend over tea, talking about everything under the sun: relationships, sex, work, books, movies, dying parents, sick loved ones, personal health issues. You name it, and women talk about it! The only problem is finding the time; and that means making the time.

Grace Note

Put down this book and go call your friend. Make a date. Better yet, call a few friends and invite them over for brunch this weekend. Go ahead. I'll still be here when you get back. . . . Now, don't you feel better? Isn't it nice to have something to look forward to? Therein lies the grace, that little smile that's coming to your face right now as you think about getting together with your friends and laughing until it hurts? That grace is precious, and it can't be quantified or measured. But it can be misplaced or set aside because you're too busy or too tired. Remember that your friendships feed you on a deeper level—a soul level. Understand that you need that juicy, tasty bite, even if it's only for half an hour. Recognize that you need that savory connection to life, to the things that really matter, because that's what carries you through the hard times. That's what lifts you up when you're down. That's what allows you to laugh in the face of the worst that life can hit you with. That is your grace.

Sacred Circles

In the wake of declining religious affiliations, women are seeking out spiritual connections in less formal settings, such as artists' and writers' groups, healing circles, and yoga classes. These are all forms of the Sacred Circle, which returns women to the roots of their experience, awakens a connection to the natural cycle of life in ways their 9-to-5 routines don't allow for, and brings women back to their core identity. Sacred Circles are the portals through which women connect to ancient rites and rituals—the moon lodge, the wisdom circle, the menstrual rites, and the marriage bed. All of these major events in a woman's life used to be celebrated, honored, and marked with ceremony. Not that we need to return to the magical thinking of a past era or to the fetishes of ancient tribal rites. But we do need to find a meaningful, modern way to come together as women, as healers, as mothers, as sisters and daughters and as friends to honor each other, serve each other, and uplift each other.

The Artist's Way[39] began a movement to reinvent the Sacred Circle by challenging women to explore creative expression as a path toward self-awareness and a more meaningful life. Other leading authors and activists include Sark and Marianne Williamson, Pema Chodron and Sharon Salzberg, and media figures like Oprah Winfrey. Each one of them has made strides in leading women toward a path to their highest Self.

My first experience of a Sacred Circle came from one of my earliest yoga classes. A group of us decided to meet early in the mornings to chant and meditate. We were a small group of five or six dedicated practitioners who met once a week. From that experience, I gained a teacher, a dear friend, and a life-long dedication to devotional music. I went on to lead chanting circles (*kirtans*) in that same community,

---

39 More information about Julia Cameron's books and workshops can be found at www.theartistsway.com.

and I continue to use music to bring people together and build relationships all around the world. I've also been a participant in artists' circles, writing circles, healing circles, full moon circles, and more. Each of these experiences has brought a richness to my life and my experience as a woman. Each of these experiences has brought me deeper to the truth of my own nature. Each of these experiences has brought me closer to the sisterhood that we as women share—shared values, shared experiences, shared creativity, and the common hope for peace, prosperity, and happiness.

Grace Note

Close your eyes and breathe deeply. With your mind's eye, surround yourself with all the women in your life—friends, family, sisters, mothers, daughters, teachers. Include any feminine spirit guides you may have, such as Mary, St. Claire, Gaia, Saraswati, Tara, Crow Medicine, or Turtle Medicine. Join hands with them all and form a circle. Observe their faces, their expressions; open your sensory awareness to the vibration you hold together. Some of these relationships may have been challenging; some perhaps still are. Whatever the vibration—good or bad—shift it to gratitude. Tune in to the gifts they have brought you and experience the gifts you bring to them. Look into each one of their eyes and give thanks. This is your Sacred Circle. This is your circle of life. These faces, past and future, are your journey to being the woman you are today. Rejoice and bless them all. Meditate on this Sacred Circle any time you feel alone; any time you need support, surround yourself with the light of consciousness and with the grace of your feminine Sacred Circle. They are your grace.

Another experience of the Sacred Circle that has stayed with me all these years was a vision I received during a shamanic healing session. In the vision, my hair was being combed and oiled by an elder woman and a young girl, as though I were being prepared for some sacred journey. I was then surrounded by a circle of women dressed in white, with long flowing hair, who were weeping, begging me to return home. I was then surrounded by a white light as two dogs came to attack me. They were ferocious, rabid, but they couldn't penetrate the light to reach me. Within months of this vision, I moved to northern New Mexico, where I'm surrounded by women with long hair who dress in white! Of course, the vision isn't quite that literal, but I often return to it as I meditate on the meaning of being here, being part of an intentional community, a Sacred Circle of practitioners who constantly battle the rabid dogs of ego and selfishness. Those dogs don't go away just because you make a decision to live consciously; in fact, they often become more pronounced as your will is tested by habits and unconscious agendas. Living in community is complicated. It's not always pretty. Human beings, living together, come with conflicts and differences of opinion. It's natural. It's human nature. The negotiation of self-interest, along with the greater good of the community, is an ongoing enterprise that must constantly be attended to, nursed, and managed.

The art of community lies in tolerance, mutual respect, and individual sovereignty, all balanced by the needs and interests of the commonwealth. Community building truly is an art, a skill acquired through experience, observation, and study. Humans have been negotiating community for thousands of years, if not hundreds of thousands of years.[40] We've swung from totalitarianism to anarchy and back again—all in an effort to figure out the best ways to live

---

40 See the research and speculation regarding Ardi and the advent of new discoveries that reinforce intimacy, connection and community in the pre-historic human era: www.nationalgeographic.com.

with each other. "Man is a social animal,"[41] so we can't avoid it. Those who've glorified the Old West and who long to return to the absolute ideals of individualism and a "bootstraps" mentality will never survive in the new Age, where community is paramount.

Selfless Service

Another approach to community building, and probably the most productive, is service. Extending your hand to your neighbor does more to build community than anything else. The return to community values and volunteerism—all forms of philanthropy—are on the rise again. It's due in part to the economic insecurity; but it's also an awakening of values that first surfaced 40 years ago. Crushed by the political and social constructs of the period, those values and ideals brought about great changes; but they also brought about tremendous backlash. Today we're seeing them return, but in a friendlier climate that recognizes their universal values and contributions to community building, peacemaking, and ultimately a cultural sea change for the better.

Helping others ranks among the highest predictors for personal happiness. Evidently, craven selfishness has met its natural end. Science is confirming what people have known for years: The isolation and loneliness that make up a large part of the American experience can't change by sitting in front of the TV. It can only change by reaching out. Community service is one of the major keys to happiness in modern life. Whether it's your local food and clothing drive, a 5K run, a bake sale for the community playground, organizing an event for a regional fundraiser, volunteering for a political campaign, or working on the national level to raise

41 Attributed to Aristotle, whose actual quote was "man is a political animal." However, his sentiments as expressed in this quote from *Politics* infer the traditional attribution: "He who is unable to live in society, or who has no need because he is sufficient for himself, must be either a beast or a god; he is no part of a state."

consciousness about a cause you believe in, these simple acts not only help others but also make you feel better. This is one case where self-interest can serve the greater good! We all want to feel better, right?

In a way, community building and service are the most viable means for living out our purpose. For many of us, work is simply that—work. It's not our calling. Serving the causes we most believe in, however, can be the most fulfilling parts of our lives—more than our jobs could ever be. What's your passion? Look around. What ways—large or small—can you apply that passion to your own community and make a difference? Maybe it's as simple as a clean-up-the-neighborhood project or as complex as a long-term program for middle school girls to succeed in school and go on to college. Live your passion and let your passion live. This is your grace.

Making a difference in other people's lives doesn't always come from volunteering in formal environments or service projects. Sometimes it's just through your day-to-day relationships. Your neighbor's son, your daughter's best friend, your mother's daytime caregiver; the list could go on. You touch these people's lives each and every day. Is your touch binding people together? Uplifting them to their destiny? Confirming their value? My own mother is the perfect example of this kind of service. When I was growing up, she didn't do much formal community service other than her involvement in her church, which was considerable; but everyone who knew her was touched by her kindness, her respect, and her compassion. Countless friends have come up to me over the years, thanking me for sharing my parents with them, reporting that a conversation with my father or a confrontation by my mother had changed the course of their lives. My parents saw people where they were, even as they held them up to a higher standard, which gave people the strength and the courage to be better than they thought they could be. My parents elevated people, without judgment and with great compassion; they repeatedly encouraged and supported people to be their best. As the child of such esteemed people, the challenge to be the best often weighed heavily; but in the end, how can I not be grateful for the blessings they brought into people's lives—my own and others? Be that difference in someone's life. That's your grace.

In an increasingly polarized world, how can we hope to transform war into peace, scarcity into abundance, and hate into love? Women are the key. Mothers who've lost their sons to war; women who've been raped at the hands of the enemy; daughters who've witnessed their father's powerlessness; if these women, who've experienced the worst that the human experience has to offer, can forgive, then there is hope. We see examples of this living hope all around the world: Truth and Reconciliation in South Africa and Central America; Palestinian and Jewish unity movements in Israel; Iranian women speaking up for political and social rights; the list goes on. These sacred circles of human beings reaching out to heal other human beings—even those who have harmed them—represent the transformative nature of relationships and a new culture of acceptance of the human condition.

When we drop our defenses and tune in to the essence of these teachings—be your Self—we begin to relax. In that relaxed state, we sense the limitless, infinite, creative power that lies within us as women. That power is what will change the world in the coming Aquarian Age. Yogi Bhajan said that the Aquarian Age would not manifest without these teachings. So, it is up to us as women to lead the world to prosperity and peace. It is up to us to deliver the fruits of the Aquarian Age—creativity, community, transparency, and reliance upon Infinity.

But before we can lead, we must master our own inner conflicts and duality. We must recognize that our security doesn't come from anything outside ourselves. It can only come from within; it can only come from our connection to the Infinite. We must acknowledge that we can only contain our world—not control it. But that simple act of prayerfully holding the world together— the epitome of the Adi Shakti—is our greatest virtue. We must know—deep in our bones—that we are the creators. Look around; if you don't like what you see, change! Change yourself! The fruit of that consciousness will seed itself throughout the world in peace, prosperity, and grace.

The most profound way for a woman to lead is by simply being herself—the graceful woman she is. Yes, she is the head of state, negotiating peace. She is the president of corporations, leading business to new standards in ethical practices, green production processes, and social progress. She is the entrepreneur, bringing agility and flexibility to the marketplace. She is the artist, transforming the way people see each other. She is the singer, opening the hearts of all who hear her. She is the architect, designing the way we live. She is the scientist, discovering new medicines, new galaxies, new formulas. She is the mother who devotes everything, selflessly, for her children. She is the sister or the daughter who holds your hand and tells you silly jokes while you wait for the doctor. She is the wife who challenges, inspires, serves, and loves you. Yes, she is; and to borrow a now-famous phrase, "Yes, she can." Women are the leaders of the Aquarian Age not because they have finally "won" the proverbial war of the sexes, but instead because they have finally recognized their own true nature and decided to serve it—and deliver it—for the good of all.

Chapter Ten

Saving Grace

What happens to one woman happens to all the women of the world. If you understand this consciousness, then you can begin to make things right.[42]

—*Yogi Bhajan*

You don't hear it very often anymore, but in the past, you would often hear men refer to their wives or partners by saying, "She's my saving grace." We've reached a point in our world where it's incumbent upon us to teach our sons and daughters; it's time to call upon our husbands and fathers and brothers; it's time to call on them to defend our grace—the grace of all women, everywhere. We've come to a point in our society where we need those same men to stand up and begin "saving grace"—literally. It's time to begin standing up for women's rights here and around the world.

42 © The Teachings of Yogi Bhajan, July 9, 1979

It's time we recognize the beauty, radiance, and creativity that is our gift—to our Self and everyone around us. Accept our nature—good and bad—and be ready to step into the Aquarian Age as a graceful women, the gift of God. If we hope to have a future that will sustain all of us in prosperity and peace, then we must begin to apply the principle introduced in the first few pages of this book: "What is good for women is good for everyone." Women are the living grace, the living face of the Divine on this planet. We are the saving grace of the entire world.

We live in a world where women are regularly subjected to violence. Each and every day, women are abused, beaten, raped, and killed—by men—as tools of war. Each and every day women are exploited, sexually and emotionally—by men—as tools of commerce. We live in a world in which women are complicit in this exploitation, in ways both conscious and unconscious: women who circumcise other women; women who don't protect their daughters; women who use their bodies, their beauty, their sexuality to get ahead. The deep subconscious phobias that lie at the heart of this violence by men against women—and the systematic self-hatred that lies at the heart of this betrayal by women against women—can be addressed and healed.

There is a prayer—a song really—written by a saint, who, with his musician and friend, traveled and sang about the ecstasy of knowing, loving, and being one with the Divine. He sang a song in praise of the woman as the manifestation of the Divine. This song heals the mother phobia and anger in both men and women by helping each to recognize the beauty and bounty of woman. Everything comes from woman, and this prayer allows the mind and the heart to both honor and rest in this truth: from woman all things come.

Grace Note

Take a moment to sit with this song, line by line. Meditate. Call to mind all the women in your life. As you meditate on your mother, your beloved, your daughters and sisters and friends, see each of their faces. Allow the emotions to arise; it's okay if they are not all positive. Just breathe; and as each new face comes into your mind's eye, bless that person. Inhale deeply and send your prayer out on the exhale. Even if the relationship is broken, send out a blessing on the breath. Now imagine all the women around the world who have suffered at the hand of violence. Now imagine all the men who've generated that violence. Send this prayer out to them—the broken and those who've broken them—that they may experience the truth of this prayer, the gift of the woman, and be healed of their anger and fear. May this prayer return women to their rightful place of honor; may woman be respected and protected; and may our world be healed and come to know a profound peace and prosperity in the Aquarian Age. This is grace.

From Woman

From woman, man is born
Within woman, man is conceived
To woman, he is engaged and married.
Woman becomes his friend and
Through woman, the future generations come.
When his woman dies, he seeks another woman—
To woman, he is bound.
Why call her bad? From whom kings are born.
From woman, woman is born
Without woman, there would be no one.
O Nanak, only the True One is without a woman.
That mouth, which praises the Lord continually, is blessed and beautiful.
O Nanak, their faces shall be radiant in the Court of the True Lord.

~Guru Nanak Dev Ji, Bhand Jammee-ai

Activism Around the World

All around the world, women are standing up for other women, standing up for themselves, and standing up for grace. Whether fighting for equal rights in Iran or access to education in Afghanistan and Pakistan, or fighting against physical mutilation in Continental Africa or the sex-slave trade in Southeast Asia, women all around the world are standing up against oppression—and standing up for their mothers, their sisters, their daughters, and future generations. A few men have joined in the fight as well.

It is in the fundamental issues regarding women's rights—access to education, health care, and rights to determine their own bodies—that the pervasive misogyny is seen in its most raw form, its starkest expression. But even in developed countries, women continue to have to fight for the right to make decisions about their own bodies and their own lives, each and every day. The art of being a woman means fighting for and obtaining those rights, with our personal integrity and grace intact. We can gain all the rights in the world, but if we are no longer women, if we lose what is essential to our nature, what have we gained?

The women's movement in Iran is a beautiful example. It has no formal organization, leadership, or nongovernmental organization status, because women are not allowed to organize there. However, Iran legalized a woman's status to vote and participate in parliament long before many other industrialized cultures, and women in Iran continue to outnumber men in higher education—both in enrollment and in professorships. Contrast that with a woman's rights in Iran today: The country's draconian, misogynist laws allow men to marry up to four wives at a time, to divorce at will, and to engage their daughters to marry as young as age 13, without any consent of the mother. She's not allowed to travel without the permission of her husband; she has no legal rights over her children; and forget about divorce or protecting herself against attackers. In fact, a woman who kills her attacker in the act of rape is charged with murder; men, on the other hand, have very little culpability because the law—God's law, no less—is on their side. Even a woman's value—her "blood price"—is half the reimbursement of a man's! This is clearly counter to the reality we know through the Teachings of Yogi Bhajan, in which a woman's worth is priceless.

In the 1950s and 1960s, Iran had one of the most modern, progressive cultures in the world. Women were making headway in leadership and government positions as well. Then the Islamic Revolution turned an entire generation and society on its head. Shirin Ebadi, lawyer, activist, and Nobel Peace Prize winner, is the daughter of that revolution. One of the founders of the One Million Signatures Campaign for Equality in Iran, she has been fighting for the rights of Iranian children and mothers for more than 20 years. She and others like her in Iran are standing up for themselves—and the men of Iran are beginning to stand up for them as well. As I write, the uprising after the 2009 presidential election continues. Women and men of Iran continue to gather in the streets, demanding to be heard. And their voices are carrying throughout the region, into Afghanistan, Pakistan, and beyond.

Recent photos and stories surrounding the acid attack of Afghani school girls by local Taliban men are horrifying and serve as evidence of the systemic brutalization of women and girls on a daily basis in Afghanistan. Even more recently, activist Sitara Achikzai was martyred in that country. The popularity of Greg Mortenson's *Three Cups of Tea* brought these events into the public discourse, and great progress has been made in the more than 15 years that he and his nonprofit, Central Asia Institute (CAI), have been in Pakistan. But there is very little political will to make the kinds of changes that would inform a long-term cultural shift in Afghanistan—a shift that would uplift and support women in their rights to education, health care, and political participation. Still, Mortenson's work in Pakistan has shown that girls who receive even a fifth-grade education have fewer unwanted pregnancies and more opportunities for success. They create small businesses, educate their own children, and, in general, bring greater prosperity and peace to their local communities. The education of young girls is what is known in the military as a "force multiplier"—that is, the investment in girls is multiplied countless times in the benefits that the family, the village, and, ultimately, the state receive in return for their investment. Once again, this provides evidence toward our recurrent theme, "What is good for women is good for everyone."

Another major movement in Africa and the Middle East is the anti–female circumcision movement. This barbaric practice, also known as female genital mutilation, continues throughout Africa and the Middle East. In fact, up until the 1950s, variations of this practice even existed in the southern states of the United States. I've been aware of this issue since I was a young woman. My first exposure came from stories of my father's experience in Tanzania. His harrowing tale of the first delivery he supported as a field doctor in the mountains of central Tanzania has stayed with me all these years. He described the shock of seeing a woman's external genitalia having been completely removed: an almost extinct version of female mutilation in which not only the clitoris is removed, but also the outer and inner labia. He undraped her lower body to deliver the child, only to discover a gaping hole where her labia should have been—skin as taut as a drum stretched over her pubic bone and vaginal opening. Heartbreaking. Variations of the practice continue even today and are the most chilling examples of women's complicity in the patriarchal suppression and oppression of other women—even their own children. Excision is done by women to other women—girls really—in order to make them more "eligible" for marriage.

My second introduction to this brutal practice came from Alice Walker's novel *Possessing the Secret of Joy*, which she later followed with a nonfiction book titled *Warrior Marks*, which explores, in-depth, the history and practice of female genital mutilation. Her novels exposed the practice to a broader American reading audience. Activism continues around the world to not only reduce the dangers associated with this practice but also to stop the practice altogether, as well as the cultural taboos that accompany it.

Another major problem in Africa, AIDS, combines with poverty and a lack of education to compound the rising tide of childhood slavery, often as child sex workers. As long as humans have existed, the oldest profession has followed them. Prostitution is endemic and will remain so as long as women and men are willing to continue selling themselves or their children. Today, however, sexual slavery is a plague in low-income countries. Throughout the world, girls are sold into sexual slavery. This practice has achieved record levels of corruption throughout Southeast Asia and parts of India and Africa. Increased sex tourism by the West, along with drought, famine, and the AIDS epidemic, has escalated childhood sexual slavery around the world. In fact, current statistics indicate that slavery is more widespread and pervasive than at any other time in human history! It simply has a different face.

Another major problem that women of the world face today is the repercussions of war. Some women and children have survived war for generations and have never known peace. Stasa Zajovic, founder of Women in Black, along with the founders of Project Air in Rwanda, are attempting to bring healing and catharsis to women in war-torn countries. Now, whether through civil, peaceful protest or therapeutic yoga, women are beginning to transform their experiences of violence into inner peace and equanimity.

Women around the world, along with the pioneering women here in the West, such as Sojourner Truth, Rosa Parks, and Margaret Sanger, have been making a difference, one woman at a time, for years. Their actions, taken in consciousness, have served to advance women's interests in their own lifetime and in the generations that followed them. Take the next step—make a difference in your own communities. Reach out to that young woman you see at the grocery store each day who has one too many children in diapers and could use your help; extend a hand to that young girl you see struggling to make it at the local community college; give what you can to the local homeless women's shelter. Whatever you're called to do—begin. This is your grace.

Sisterhood of Grace

"What's good for women is good for everyone" is a truth we can all carry in our hearts and our minds—a truth we can carry into the world as we serve our brothers and sisters within our own communities or beyond our own borders. Grace is the wisdom to see beyond ourselves. Grace is the kindness to lend a hand. Grace is patience in the face of adversity. Grace is healing in the midst of pain and sorrow. Grace is endurance in the wake of suffering. Grace is peace within the throes of war. Grace is light in all the shadowy places.

Grace Note

Meditate on your own grace. Open your mind and your heart to the reality of your Self and your presence as the Grace of God. Sit with that reality and begin to manifest it in your thoughts, your expressions, your mannerisms, your actions. Visualize your Self as the Grace of God. See yourself, in your everyday life, living out your everyday grace. What does it mean to be the Grace of God at the local grocer's market? At the bank teller's window? During your commute? At your local community center? When your children come home from school? As your husband or partner walks through the door? What does it mean to bring grace to everything you touch? See it. Be it. The Grace of God.

Blessed be the woman. Her grace is the face of God here on Earth. She is the radiant Divine Light; her touch is the long-awaited healing; her smile brings laughter; her voice, a solace; her wisdom manifests every good thing—prosperity, happiness, and peace—here on Earth. Blessed be. Blessed be. Blessed be the woman. "For what is good for the woman is good for everyone."

The Grace of God Movement
and the Teachings of Yogi Bhajan

The "movement" that these teachings reflect began from one man's devotion; one man's understanding of the power of a mother's prayer; one man's recognition of the Divine within himself as a gift from his mother. Yogi Bhajan came here in 1969, at the height of the cultural and sexual revolutions in the United States. But where we thought we were experiencing "freedom," he saw only exploitation. Gail Collins, in her new historical survey of the women's movement since 1960, *When Everything Changed*, mirrors Yogi Bhajan's observations: With the advent of the "pill," women who had traditionally been seen in the role of wife and mother, sister and daughter, were now free to be seen and exploited as purely sexual objects. The pill didn't invent the exploitation of women, but it certainly took it one step further.

Yogi Bhajan arrived on the heels of this "revolution" and determined to spend the rest of his days teaching women how to be women; he dedicated his life to uplifting women toward their grace, reminding them of their invincibility, and pointing them toward their Divinity, their sacred Mother Nature. He sincerely believed in the power of woman to affect those changes we all longed to see—peace, harmony, and prosperity—throughout the world. We still long for that change! Yet he believed it could only manifest through woman and her creativity. He believed in the promise of a graceful woman's children; he believed in the courage and integrity of a graceful woman's husband; he believed in woman—her invincibility and her strength.

He often spoke about women and the Aquarian Age, saying that we would only manifest the promise of this Age through the technology of the graceful woman. He came here to deliver that technology—and for more than 25 years, he did just that. He spent six weeks every summer, from 1976 until his health no longer allowed him to, teaching and elevating hundreds of women who came to study, heal, and become the leaders and teachers of today and tomorrow.

Women represent the hope of the future. Through their prayer, through their children, through their grace, the world will shift so that once again, we can "get back to the garden." My prayer is that this book will be a first step in your exploration of your Self as the Grace of God—a woman of compassion, kindness, and peace; a woman of strength, integrity, and justice. Put simply, just a woman.

Everyday Recipes

Ms. Whiz Recipe: The Perfect Morning Drink

1 ripe banana

8 ounces (250 ml) orange juice

1 Tablespoon (20 ml) liquid chlorophyll

2 Teaspoons Rice Bran Syrup

2 Teaspoons cold-pressed almond or sesame oil

Blend well until frothy.

Golden Milk

This recipe provides both vital ingredients—essential oils and turmeric—to help women keep their flexibility and vitality in the tissues. The oil provides lubrication and energy to the system, while turmeric makes the bones and joints more flexible.

1/8 teaspoon Turmeric

2 Tablespoons Almond Oil

1/2 cup water

8 oz whole dairy milk

honey to taste

Optional: one cardamom pod

Boil turmeric in water for 8 minutes. Meanwhile bring milk and almond oil to boil. When the milk is boiling, turn off the heat and add the turmeric mixture to the milk and serve with honey to taste. The turmeric should completely surrender to the water. The cardamom seeds may be cooked with the turmeric for added flavor, but they are optional.

The Original Yogi Tea

For each 8 oz. cup, start with 10 oz. of water. (Recommended: Make a minimum of 4 cups at a time.) The measurements can vary according to your taste; but be sure to not put in too many cloves or cinnamon sticks.

To each cup of boiling water add:

3 whole cloves
4 whole cardamom pods
4 whole black peppercorns
½ stick cinnamon

Continue boiling for at least 15 minutes or up to an hour, then add:

1/4 tsp. of any black tea. Let it sit for about one minute, and then add:

1/2 cup cold dairy milk (per cup of liquid)[43]

When it reaches the boiling point, remove immediately from the heat. Strain and serve with honey to taste.

---

43 Many people these days replace milk with other 'milks' (that is, soy, rice or other); but these milk replacements do not serve the digestive system in the same way, and therefore cannot replace milk in the Original Yogi Tea Recipe. Raw Yogi Tea, made without the milk, is an alternate way of serving Yogi Tea, which allows for alternate 'milk' options.

Kitcheri

A perfectly balanced protein dish, easy to digest, and very satisfying—makes a great monodiet. Good any time of the year, but makes a particularly good winter diet, or when recovering from an illness.

4-1/2 cups Water

1/2 cup Mung Beans

1/2 cup Basmati Rice

1/4 cup Ginger Root, finely minced

1 Onion, chopped

3 cloves Garlic, minced

3 cups chopped Vegetables

2 Tablespoons (40 ml) Ghee or Vegetable Oil

3/4 teaspoon Turmeric

1/4 teaspoon crushed Red Chilies

1/4 teaspoon ground Black Pepper

1/2 teaspoon ground Coriander

1/2 teaspoon ground Garam Masala

1/2 teaspoon ground Cumin

1/4 teaspoon Cardamom Seeds (2 pods)

1 Bay Leaf

Rinse mung beans and rice. Add mung beans to boiling water and cook until beans begin to split. Add rice and cook another 15 minutes, stirring occasionally. Now add the vegetables. As the mixture cooks, it will start to thicken.

Heat the ghee or vegetable oil in a frying pan. Add onions, ginger, and garlic and sauté until clear. Add spices and cook 5 more minutes, stirring constantly. Add this to the rice and beans. The final consistency should be like a thick soup. Total cooking time is about 1-1/2 hours. Add salt or soy sauce to taste. Serve plain or with yogurt. Makes 4 servings.

Everyday Asanas for Women

Butterfly Pose
Baddha Konasana

- Begin in Easy Pose.
- Grab underneath the feet, and hold the soles of the feet together.
- Pull the spine up.
- Apply neck lock.
- Bounce the knees, coordinate with the breath.
- Great for pregnancy!

Camel Pose
Ustrasana

- Begin by sitting on the heels and rise up onto the knees.
- Root yourself with the knees, pressing firmly into the earth.
- Bring the pelvis forward, tilt the tailbone under, lift the heart center, and exhale as you lean back.
- Lift the hips as high as you can.
- Grab the heels or ankles.
- Drop the head back.

Cat Stretch

- Begin by lying on the back.
- Stretch the arms out to the sides.
- Keeping the shoulders on the ground, pull up one knee and bend it over to the opposite side of the body on the ground.
- Do the same with the other leg.

Cat-Cow
Marjariasana

- Begin on the hands and knees.
- The hands are shoulder-width apart, with fingers facing forward. The knees are directly under the hips.
- Inhale and tilt the pelvis forward, arching the spine down (cow position), with head and neck stretched back. Do not scrunch the neck. Open the heart and raise the chin as far back as you can without collapsing the neck.

Cat-Cow *(continued)*

- Exhale and tilt the pelvis the opposite way, arching the spine up (cat position), pressing the chin into the chest.
- Start off slowly, then when the movement is established, you can speed up.
- Great for pregnancy!

Cobra Pose
Bhujangasana

- Begin by lying on the stomach.
- Hands under the shoulders, palms flat on the ground.
- Lift the chest and heart up first, and let the head follow as you lean back.
- Straighten the arms.
- Modified: If you can't keep your feet together, keep the back of the upper thighs together. If it is difficult to keep your arms straight, bend your elbows, or put your forearms on the ground.

Crow Pose

- Begin in a standing position.
- Squat down. Knees and feet are wide apart, with heels flat on the ground.
- Apply Neck Lock.
- Stretch the arms in front of you for balance.
- If you are having difficulty getting down, or keeping your balance, try widening the feet and knees more.
- If you can't get the heels down, you may use something underneath your feet.
- Great for pregnancy!

Frog Pose

- Squat down on the toes.
- The heels are lifted off the ground and touching.
- Place the fingertips on the ground between the legs.
- The face is forward.
- Inhale as you raise the hips up, keeping the fingertips on the ground, heels up, knees locked.
- Exhale down; face is forward, knees outside the arms.

Gyan Mudra (Seal of Knowledge)

The most commonly used mudra.
Sit in Easy Sitting Pose and put
the tip of the thumb together with
the tip of the index finger. This
stimulates knowledge, wisdom, and
the power to compute. The energy
of the index finger is associated with
Jupiter, representing expansion. It
gives receptivity and calmness.

Life Nerve Stretch (Front Stretch)

Paschimottanasana

- Begin by sitting down, with the legs stretched out in front.
- Grab the big toes in finger lock. (Index finger and middle finger pull the toe, and the thumb presses the nail of the toe.)
- Exhale, lengthening the spine, bending forward from the navel, continuing to lengthen the spine.
- Inhale, use the legs to push up.
- The head follows last. Don't lead with the head.
- Try to get the belly to the thighs rather than the head to the knees.
- Engage the thighs for a better stretch.
- Yogi Bhajan called this stretch the 'test of the woman', that is, your elbows should be able to touch the ground on each side of your thighs.
- Variation: Legs spread wide. Follow instructions in the kriya.

Pelvic Lifts

Kandharasana

- Lie on the back.
- Bend the knees. Feet are flat on the ground.
- Grab hold of the ankles.
- Inhale, engage the navel, and lift the hips up.
- Exhale down.
- Focus on opening the Heart Cente
- Great for pregnancy!

Rock Pose

Vajrasana

- Sit on the heels.
- Pull a light neck lock.
- Great for digestion!

Spinal Flex (Camel Ride)

- Sit in Easy Pose.
- Grab the ankles or shins.
- Root the sitting bones into the ground.
- Inhale and rock the pelvis forward, pulling the chin into the throat to open up the spine. Push the chest forward and up.
- Exhale, round the lower back, rocking the pelvis back.
- Keep the head in a slight Neck Lock so that it doesn't move up and down.
- Variation: Spinal Flex is sometimes done in Rock Pose, sitting on the heels.

Torso Twist

- Sit in Easy Pose or Rock Pose, on the heels.
- Grab the shoulders, with the thumbs in back, and other fingers in front.
- Inhale, twist to the left.
- Exhale, twist to the right.
- Rotate from the Navel Point.
- Chin in Neck Lock; the head moves with the torso.
- In Spinal Twist, Yogi Bhajan instructs that we only inhale twisting left, exhale twisting right. We don't reverse the breath.

Sat Kriya

- Sit on the heels.
- Clasp the hands above thehead, with fingers interlaced except for the index fingers, which point straight up. Men cross the right thumb over the left; women cross left thumb over right.
- The arms are straight, hugging the ears.
- Squeeze the Navel Point in and up as you say "sat (sut)." Do not snap the Navel Point.
- Release on the sound "naam".
- Do not move the pelvis or the spine as in Spinal Flex.

Shoulder Stand

Salamba Sarvangasana

- Bring the hips and legs up to vertical position, making spine and legs perpendicular to the ground.
- Place the hands on the hips, just below the waist, and keep your elbows parallel to each other.
- Make sure your weight is supported by the shoulders, not the neck.

Shoulder Shrugs

- Sit in Easy Pose or in Rock Pose, on the heels.
- Place the hands on the knees.
- Inhale, and bring the shoulders up to the ears.
- Exhale, and release them down.
- Move rapidly.
- Variation: Some kriyas call for raising alternate shoulders.

Stretch Pose

- Lie on the back with the feet together.
- Flatten the lower back into the ground.
- Put the hands wherever it feels most natural, either palms facing the thighs alongside the body, or hands over the thighs, palms down.
- Lift the head up by lifting the heart up. Apply Neck Lock and look at the toes.
- Lift the feet up 6 inches.
- Begin Breath of Fire.
- Variations: You may use hands under the buttocks to support the lower back. Or, you may use one leg at a time, but keep the Breath of Fire powerful.
- Avoid when pregnant!

Sufi Grind

- Sit in Easy Pose.
- Grab hold of the knees and move the spine in a big circle.
- Inhale as the body rotates forward.
- Exhale as you rotate backwards.
- The head stays above the pelvis and the spine flexes as it moves.

Keeping the Body Beautiful

1. Long Deep Breathing

Sit in Easy Pose with spine straight. Begin breathing long and deep through both nostrils. Focus on the life-giving flow of breath for 3 minutes. To end, inhale, suspend the breath a few seconds, then relax the breath.

2. Frog Pose

Squat down on the toes, knees wide apart. Heels are touching, and raised up off the ground. Place the fingertips on the ground between the knees. The face is forward. Inhale as you raise the hips up (2a), keeping the fingertips on the ground, heels up, knees locked.

2. **Frog Pose** *(continued)*

Exhale down (2b), face forward, knees outside of arms. **10 times**. On the tenth, stay down and take three deep breaths. On the third breath exhale completely and suspend the breath out as you apply *mulbandh*. Suspend the breath out 10-20 seconds.

Repeat Frog Pose 26 times. On the last time, stay down and take three deep breaths. On the third breath, suspend the breath out and again apply *mulbandh*. Feel energy rise along the spine as you suspend the breath out. Do not strain.

3. **Front Stretch**

Stretch the legs out straight in front. Relax forward and grab the big toes in Finger Lock (Index finger and middle finger pull the toe, and the thumb presses on the toe.) Inhale, lengthening the spine. Exhale, bend forward from the navel, bringing chest to thighs, nose to knees. The head follows last. Avoid leading with the head. Hold the position for **3 minutes**.

Bibliography
and Recommended Reading List

Many of these books have informed my writing and my experience as a woman over the years. Although this work is based primarily on the Teachings of Yogi Bhajan, these other authors have influenced my experience as a woman and my writing in general. May they be a source of information, inspiration, and challenge as you continue on your journey toward Everyday Grace and The Art of Being a Woman.

Angier, Natalie, *Woman: An Intimate Geography* (New York: Anchor Books, 2000)

Bhajan, Yogi, *Foods for Health and Healing* (Santa Cruz, NM: Kundalini Research Institute, 1983)

Chodron, Pema, *When Things Fall Apart* (Boston: Shambala Publications, 1997)

Collins, Gail, *When Everything Changed: The Amazing Journey of American Women From 1960 to the Present* (New York: Little, Brown and Company, 2009)

Ensler, Eve, *The Vagina Monologues* (New York: Villard Books, 2008)

Goldberg, Natalie, *Writing Down the Bones: Freeing the Writer Within* (Boston: Shambala Publications, 1986, 2005)

Khalsa, Sat Purkh Kaur (ed.), *I AM A WOMAN: Creative, Sacred & Invincible* (Santa Cruz, NM: Kundalini Research Institute, 2009)

Khalsa, Sat Purkh Kaur (ed.), *Man to Man* (Santa Cruz, NM: Kundalini Research Institute, 2008)

Kristof, Nicholas D., and Sheryl WuDunn, *Half the Sky: Turning Oppression into Opportunity for Women Worldwide* (New York: Borzoi Books, 2009)

Maushart, Susan, *The Mask of Motherhood: How Becoming a Mother Changes Our Lives and Why We Never Talk About It* (New York: Penguin Books, 2000)

Northrup, Christiane, MD, *Women's Bodies, Women's Wisdom: Creating Physical and Emotional Health and Healing* (New York: Bantam Dell, 2006)

Pitchford, Paul, *Healing Through Whole Foods* (Berkeley, CA: North Atlantic Books, 1993)

Schnarch, David, *Passionate Marriage: Keeping Love and Intimacy Alive in Committed Relationships* (New York: W.W. Norton & Company, 2009)

Ueland, Brenda, *If You Want to Write* (St. Paul, MN: Graywolf Press, 1987)

Walters, Terry, *Clean Food: A Seasonal Guide to Eating Close to the Source, 2009*

Waters, Alice, *The Art of Simple Food, 1983*

Wolf, Naomi, *The Beauty Myth: How Images of Beauty Are Used Against Women* (New York: Harper Collins, 2002)

Index

N

Naa, 52
Naam, 106
Native peoples, 100
Natural length of hair, 22
Nature of
    relationships, 11, 142
    sexuality, 41
    woman, 5, 95
Nature of man, 76, 89, 90
Nature, 101
Navajo Prayer, 31
Navajo, 100
Navel Point, 45, 58, 69, 70, 71, 113
Neck, 44
Need
    for security, 9
    of group, 133
Needs, 90
    of men, 90
Negative self talk, 72
Negativity, 117
    and women, 73
Nerves, 74
Nervous system, 58, 110
Neuralgia, 24
Neutral mind, 81
New Age, 116
New Mexico, 100
Nighttime feedings, 111
Nipple to nipple, 16

Nipple, 16
No-fault divorce, 17
Nonviolence, 106
Normal position of the vagina, 42, 43
Notion of God, 60
Nuclear
    proliferation, 106
    weapons, 108
Nurse, 109
Nursing, 110

O

Oil, 24, 111
    almond, 24
    cold-pressed, 63
    olive, 24
    sesame, 24
Olive oil, 24
One Million Signatures Campaign for Equality in Iran, 149
One Minute Breath, 25, 26
Ong Namo Guru Dev Namo, i
Onions, 128
Oppression, 6
Orb, 15
Orgasm, 41
Ovaries, 14
Overeat, 51
"Our Deepest Fear", 10
Oxidization, 29

About the Author

Sat Purkh Kaur Khalsa is a writer, editor, poet, singer, songwriter—and a pretty good cook, too. A certified Kundalini Yoga Instructor and a Trainer in the KRI Aquarian Trainer Academy, she serves as Editor and Creative Director for the Kundalini Research Institute. Her second album, *Beautiful Day: The Aquarian Sadhana*, is available at www.kundaliniresearchinstitute.org. Her first album, *Nectar of the Name*, was released in 2007 by Spirit Voyage. She's currently working on her next two books: *Stepping into Meditation: Kundalini Yoga and the Path of Recovery* and *Pop Tart: Growing up S.A.D.* (Standard American Diet); and dreaming about her next album, *Queen Be: Mantras and Meditations on the Divine Feminine*. She lives with her two cats, Fatty and Slim, and her two dogs, Vinnie and Lily—and stacks and stacks of books.

CPSIA information can be obtained
at www.ICGtesting.com
Printed in the USA
FFHW021952040219
50435955-55615FF

9 781934 532317